Succeed at A2 Sociology

The Complete Revision Guide

✓ Provides the key knowledge and AO2 skills for exam success

✓ Advice on exam technique from senior examiners

✓ Practice questions for you to try

✓ Examples of top-grade student answers

The ONLY A2 Sociology revision book written by Chief and Principal Examiners

Designed by expert examiners to boost your grade

Rob Webb and Keith Trobe

NAPIER PRESS *Sociology*

Published by Napier Press
PO Box 6383
Brentwood
CM13 2NQ
Email: napierpress@aol.com
Website: www.sociology.uk.net

ISBN-10   0-9540079-8-0
ISBN-13   978-0-9540079-8-0
EAN   9780954007980

British Library Cataloguing in Publication Data
A catalogue record for this book is available from the British Library

Edited by Rob Webb
Design by HL Studios
Printed and bound by Vertis Group Ltd

NAPIER PRESS *Sociology*

Go to www.sociology.uk.net
On-line support for AS and A level Sociology teachers and students.

Contents

CHAPTER 1 BELIEFS IN SOCIETY

1 Theories of Religion

Key Issues
▶ What are the key features of different sociological theories of religion?
▶ How do functionalist, Marxist and feminist theories differ?
▶ What criticisms can be made of each of these theories?

Functionalist theories of religion

▶ Functionalists see society as like an organism, with basic needs that it must meet to survive. Each institution performs certain functions to maintain the social system by meeting a need.

▶ Society's most basic need is for social order and solidarity. For functionalists, what makes order possible is value consensus – a set of shared norms and values for people to follow.

▶ Durkheim (1915) argues that religious institutions play a central part in creating and maintaining value consensus, order and solidarity.

Analysis
Explain the functionalist argument that value consensus is necessary for society to hold together – without it, individual selfishness would cause social disintegration.

The sacred and the profane
For Durkheim, the key feature of all religions is a fundamental distinction between the sacred and the profane.

▶ **The sacred** are things set apart and forbidden, inspiring feelings of awe, fear and wonder, with taboos and prohibitions.

▶ **The profane** are ordinary things that have no special significance.

Rituals A religion is more than a set of beliefs: it has sacred rituals or practices and these rituals are *collective* – performed by social groups.

Application
Give examples of sacred things (e.g. a religious symbol like the Christian cross) and profane things (e.g. a streetlight).

▶ Durkheim argues that sacred things create powerful feelings in believers because they are *symbols* representing something of great power, and this thing can only be society.

▶ When people worship sacred symbols, they are worshipping society itself. For Durkheim, sacred symbols perform the essential function of uniting believers into a single moral community.

▶ Durkheim believed the essence of all religion could be found by studying its simplest form, in the simplest type of society. Thus he used studies of the Arunta, an Aboriginal Australian tribe with a clan system.

Evaluation
Durkheim did not carry out any research on the Arunta himself; all his information came from secondary sources. Furthermore, religion in the simplest society may not be the same as religion in other societies.

▶ Among the Arunta, bands of kin come together to perform ritual worship of a sacred totem. The totem is the clan's emblem, such as an animal or plant that symbolises the clan's identity. The totemic rituals venerating it reinforce the group's solidarity and sense of belonging.

▶ For Durkheim, when clan members worship their totem, they are in reality worshipping society – the totem inspires awe in the clan's members precisely because it represents the power of the group.

The collective conscience

For Durkheim, the sacred symbols represent society's *collective conscience* or *consciousness* – the shared norms, values and beliefs that make cooperation between individuals possible. Without these, society would disintegrate.

▶ Regular shared religious rituals reinforce the collective conscience and maintain social integration.

▶ Rituals also remind individuals of the power of society – without which they themselves are nothing, and to which they owe everything.

▶ Thus, religion also performs an important function for the *individual*. By making us feel part of something greater than ourselves, it strengthens us to face life's problems.

Cognitive functions of religion

Durkheim sees religion as also being the source of our cognitive capacities – our ability to reason and think conceptually.

▶ In order to think at all, we need categories such as time, space etc.

▶ Religion provides the concepts and categories we need for understanding the world and communicating with others. Durkheim and Mauss (1903) argue that religion provides basic categories such as time, space and causation – e.g. with ideas about a creator bringing the world into being at the beginning of time. For Durkheim, religion is the origin of human thought, reason and science.

Psychological functions

Malinowski (1954) argues that religion promotes solidarity by performing psychological functions for individuals, helping them cope with emotional stress that would undermine social solidarity. There are two situations where it performs this role:

▶ **Where the outcome is important but uncontrollable and uncertain** In his study of the Trobriand Islanders, Malinowski contrasts lagoon and ocean fishing. Lagoon fishing is safe but ocean fishing is dangerous and uncertain, so it is always accompanied by 'canoe magic' – rituals to ensure a safe expedition. This gives people a sense of control, which eases tension, gives them confidence to undertake hazardous tasks and reinforces group solidarity.

▶ **At times of life crises** Events such as birth, puberty, marriage and especially death are potentially disruptive changes. Malinowski argues that death is the main reason for the existence of religious belief.

Parsons: values and meaning

Parsons (1967) identifies two other essential functions of religion in modern society:

▶ **It creates and legitimates society's basic norms and values** by sacralising them (making them sacred). This promotes value consensus and social stability.

▶ **It provides a source of meaning, answering 'ultimate' questions** about life, e.g. why good people suffer. These may undermine our commitment to society's values. By answering such questions, religion helps people to adjust to adverse events and maintains stability.

Civil religion

Bellah (1970) argues that religion unifies society, especially a multi-faith society like America. What unifies American society is an overarching *civil religion* – a belief system that attaches sacred qualities to society itself. Civil religion is a faith in 'the American way of life'.

▶ Civil religion integrates society in a way that individual religions cannot. American civil religion involves loyalty to the nation-state and belief in God, both of which are equated with being a true American. It is expressed in various rituals, symbols and beliefs, e.g. the pledge of allegiance to the flag.

▶ It sacralises the American way of life and binds together Americans from many different ethnic and religious backgrounds.

Marxist theories of religion

Functionalism emphasises the positive functions religion performs, but it neglects negative aspects.

Unlike functionalists, Marxists see all societies as divided into two classes, one of which exploits the labour of the other. In modern capitalist society, the capitalist class who own the means of production exploit the working class.

This creates class conflict. Marx predicted that the working class would ultimately become aware of their exploitation and overthrow capitalism, leading to a classless society and an end to exploitation.

1 Religion as ideology

For Marxists, ideology is a belief system that distorts people's perception of reality in the interests of the ruling class.

▶ The class that controls economic production also controls the production and distribution of ideas, through institutions such as religion and the media.

▶ In Marx's view, religion operates as an ideological weapon used by the ruling class to legitimate (justify) the suffering of the poor as something inevitable and god-given. Religion misleads the poor into believing they will be rewarded in the afterlife.

▶ Such ideas create a *false consciousness* – a distorted view of reality that prevents the poor from acting to change their situation.

▶ Lenin (1870-1924) describes religion as 'spiritual gin' that confuses the working class and keeps them in their place. The ruling class use religion to manipulate the masses and keep them from attempting to overthrow capitalism by creating a 'mystical fog' that obscures reality.

▶ Religion also legitimates the power and privilege of the dominant class by making their position appear divinely ordained. Disobedience is not just illegal, but a sinful challenge to God's authority.

2 Religion and alienation

Marx (1844) also sees religion as the product of alienation – becoming separated from or losing control over something that one has produced or created.

▶ Under capitalism, workers are alienated because they do not own what they produce, have no control over the production process and in the factory-based division of labour, the worker endlessly repeats the same monotonous task.

▶ In these dehumanising conditions, religion is a form of consolation – it is '*the opium of the people. It is the sigh of the oppressed creature*'.

▶ Religion acts as an opiate to dull the pain of exploitation. Its promises of the afterlife distract attention from the true source of the suffering, namely capitalism.

▶ However, some Marxists, such as Althusser (1971), reject the concept of alienation as unscientific. This would make the concept an inadequate basis for a theory of religion.

Feminist theories of religion

Feminists see society as patriarchal – based on male domination.

▶ Religious institutions are patriarchal. They reflect and perpetuate gender inequality.

▶ Religious beliefs are patriarchal ideologies that legitimate women's subordination.

Analysis
Explain how within the Marxist view of society, religion is a feature only of class-divided society – it justifies exploitation and inequality. In an equal, classless society, there is no need for religion and it will disappear.

Evaluation
Marxism ignores positive functions of religion and some Neo-Marxists see certain forms of religion as assisting, not hindering, the development of class consciousness.

Application
Support the false consciousness argument with examples such as the Divine Right of Kings in mediaeval Europe and the caste system in India.

Interpretation
The role of religion illustrates the Marxist view of power. Religious ideas maintain the existing distribution of power and privilege in society by compensating the poor for their deprivation, e.g. by promising rewards in heaven.

Evaluation
Some feminists argue that women have not always been subordinate to men within religion; e.g. Armstrong (1993) argues that early religions often placed women at the centre.

Examples of patriarchy in religion

There are many examples of patriarchy in religion.

▶ **Religious organisations** are mainly male-dominated; e.g. Orthodox Judaism and Catholicism forbid women from becoming priests. Armstrong (1993) sees women's exclusion from the priesthoods of most religions as evidence of their marginalisation.

▶ **Places of worship** often segregate the sexes and marginalise women in acts of worship, e.g. not being allowed to preach or to read from sacred texts. Taboos that see menstruation, pregnancy and childbirth as polluting may also prevent participation.

▶ **Sacred texts** largely feature the doings of male gods and prophets and often reflect anti-female stereotypes, e.g. Eve who, in the Judaeo-Christian story of Genesis, caused humanity's fall from grace and expulsion from the Garden of Eden.

▶ **Religious laws and customs** often give women fewer rights than men, e.g. in access to divorce, dress codes etc. They may also lead to unequal treatment, e.g. genital mutilation, punishment for sexual transgressions. Many religions legitimate and regulate women's traditional domestic and reproductive role, e.g. the Catholic Church bans abortion and artificial contraception.

Religious feminism

Woodhead (2002) argues that although much traditional religion is patriarchal, this is not true of all religion. There are 'religious forms of feminism' – ways women use religion to gain greater freedom and respect.

▶ While Western feminists often see the hijab (veil) worn by Muslim women as a symbol of oppression, to the wearer it may symbolise resistance to oppression: a symbol of liberation that enables her to enter the public sphere without losing her culture and history.

▶ Women may use religion to gain status and respect for their roles within the home and family; e.g. a strongly held belief among evangelical Christians is that men must respect women.

▶ The position of women in some religions is changing, e.g. since 1992, the Church of England has admitted women to the priesthood; about a fifth of its priests are now female. Other Protestant denominations, Reform Judaism and Sikhism all allow women priests.

Interpretation
Rather than simply describing examples such as these, point out that they apply across a wide range of religions and come from all aspects of religion – beliefs, texts, laws, places of worship, hierarchies etc.

Analysis
Explain El Saadawi's (1980) argument that religious patriarchy is the result of patriarchal forms of society coming into existence in the last few thousand years and re-shaping religion.

Analysis
Explain how this gives women power to influence men's behaviour by using religion to insist that men refrain from 'macho' behaviour.

ONE TO TRY

Read Item A and answer the question that follows.

Item A Marxist views of the role of religion emphasise the way in which religion oppresses different groups in society. Marxists see religion as an ideological tool of the ruling class that legitimates inequality and creates false consciousness among the working class.

Feminists argue that religion operates in a similar way but, in their view, it is women rather than the working class who are subordinated through patriarchal religious beliefs, practices and institutions.

Question Using material from **Item A** and elsewhere, assess Marxist views of the role of religion in society. (18 marks)

Examiner's Advice You need to go beyond simply presenting all you know about different Marxist views, including neo-Marxism. You should explain how they place religion in relation to conflict in society, by identifying religion's ideological role in justifying different forms of inequality (use Item A as a starting point). You should refer to some of the evidence of religion's contribution to conflict in society. You should also refer to the differences between Marxist and other conflict views (e.g. feminism) as well as the differences between conflict and consensus theories.

2 Religion and Social Change

Key Issues

▶ What is meant by social change?

▶ How do functionalist, Marxist and Weberian theories explain the relationship between religion and change?

▶ What are the strengths and weaknesses of each of these explanations?

Religion as a conservative force

Religion can be seen as a conservative force in two different senses:

1. Conservative in the sense of 'traditional', e.g. defending traditional customs, institutions, or moral views.

2. Conservative because it functions to conserve or preserve things as they are, maintaining the status quo.

Religion's conservative beliefs

▶ Most religions have traditional conservative beliefs about moral issues and oppose changes that allow individuals more freedom; e.g. the Catholic Church forbids divorce, abortion and artificial contraception.

▶ Most religions uphold 'family values', supporting a traditional patriarchal domestic division of labour; e.g. Hinduism endorses the practice of arranged marriage.

Religion's conservative functions

Religion is also conservative in the second sense of the word – functioning to conserve or preserve things as they are. This view of religion is held by functionalists, Marxists and feminists. In different ways, they each argue that it contributes to social stability.

Religion and consensus

Functionalists see religion as a conservative force maintaining social stability and preventing disintegration, e.g. promoting social solidarity by creating value consensus and helping individuals deal with disruptive stresses.

Marxists and feminists see religion as an ideology that supports the existing social structure and as a means of social control in the interests of the powerful:

▶ **Religion and capitalism** Marx sees religion as a conservative ideology preventing social change. By legitimating or disguising inequality, it creates false consciousness in the working class and prevents revolution.

▶ **Religion and patriarchy** Feminists see religion as a conservative force because it legitimates patriarchal power and maintains women's subordination in the family and society.

Weber: religion as a force for change

Weber (1905) in *The Protestant Ethic and the Spirit of Capitalism* argues that the religious beliefs of Calvinism helped to bring about major social change – the emergence of modern capitalism in Northern Europe.

▶ Modern capitalism is unique because it is based on the systematic, efficient, rational pursuit of profit for its own sake, rather than for spending on luxuries. Weber calls this *the spirit of capitalism*.

This spirit had unconscious similarity to the Calvinists' beliefs and attitudes. Calvinism had several distinctive beliefs.

Calvinist beliefs

▶ **Predestination** God predetermines who will be saved – 'the elect' – and individuals can do nothing to change this.

▶ **Divine transcendence** God is so far above and beyond this world that no human being could possibly claim to know his will – leaving the Calvinists to feel 'an unprecedented inner loneliness'. This creates what Weber calls a *salvation panic* among Calvinists.

▶ **Asceticism** Abstinence, self-discipline and self-denial.

▶ **The idea of a vocation** or calling to serve God – but in the everyday world of work, not in a monastery. Calvinism invented this-worldly asceticism, where a vocation means constant, methodical work in an occupation.

Calvinists led an ascetic lifestyle shunning all luxury, working long hours and practising rigorous self-discipline. As a result:

1. Driven by their work ethic, they systematically accumulated wealth but did not spend it on luxuries (asceticism), instead reinvesting it in their businesses to produce further profit.

2. They prospered and came to see this as a sign of God's favour and their salvation.

Hinduism and Confucianism

Weber argued that Calvinist beliefs were only one of capitalism's causes. Certain material or economic factors were necessary, e.g. natural resources, trade, a money economy, towns, a legal system etc.

There have been other societies with some of these factors, but where capitalism did not take off, due to the lack of a religious belief system like Calvinism. For example:

▶ **Hinduism** in ancient India was an ascetic religion, but was *other-worldly* – directing followers towards the spiritual world.

▶ **Confucianism** in ancient China, although a this-worldly religion that directed its followers towards the material world, it was *not ascetic*.

Religion and social protest

Bruce (2003) is interested in the relationship between religion and social change, comparing two case studies of the role of religiously inspired protest movements in America: the civil rights movement and the New Christian Right.

The American civil rights movement

The black civil rights movement of the 1950s/60s attempted to end racial segregation as blacks were denied legal and political rights in many Southern states; e.g. schools were segregated, inter-racial marriages forbidden and blacks often excluded from voting.

▶ The movement began in 1955 and direct action through protest marches, boycotts and demonstrations followed until, in 1964, segregation was outlawed.

▶ The black clergy led by Dr Martin Luther King were the backbone of the movement, giving support and moral legitimacy to activists. They shamed whites into changing the law by appealing to their shared Christian values of equality.

Bruce sees religion in this context as an *ideological resource* – beliefs that protesters could draw on for motivation and legitimation. Religious organisations are well equipped to support protests and contribute to change, e.g. by:

▶ **Taking the moral high ground** – pointing out the hypocrisy of white clergy who supported racial segregation.

▶ **Channelling dissent**, e.g. Martin Luther King's funeral was a rallying point for the civil rights cause.

Analysis
It is important to explain how these religious ideas paralleled the ideas necessary for capitalism to develop.

Evaluation
Use Kautsky to criticise Weber for overestimating the role of ideas and underestimating economic factors in bringing capitalism into being. Kautsky argues that capitalism actually came before rather than after Calvinism.

Application
Avoid being drawn into lengthy descriptions of examples. It is more important to apply the examples, e.g. showing how Hinduism and Confucianism lacked the drive of Calvinism to systematically accumulate wealth.

Interpretation
Bruce sees the civil rights movement as an example of religion becoming involved in secular struggle and helping to bring about change.

▶ **Acting as honest broker** because they are respected by both sides in a conflict and seen as standing above 'mere politics'.

▶ **Mobilising public opinion** by campaigning for support.

The New Christian Right (NCR)

▶ The NCR is a politically and morally conservative, Protestant fundamentalist movement. It has gained prominence since the 1960s.

▶ The NCR's aims are to make abortion, homosexuality and divorce illegal and take the USA 'back to God', turning the clock back to a time before the liberalisation of American society.

▶ The NCR believes in traditional family and gender roles, campaigns for the teaching of 'creationism' and wants to ban sex education in schools.

▶ The NCR uses televangelism, where church-owned TV stations raise funds and broadcast programmes aimed at making converts.

▶ The Moral Majority, a right-wing Christian pressure group and part of the NCR, became the focus for political campaigning and for influencing the Republican Party.

Bruce argues that the NCR has been largely unsuccessful because it has never had the support of more than 15% of the population at most. The democratic values of American society mean most Americans are comfortable with legalising activities such as abortion and homosexuality.

Marxism, religion and change

Marxists are often thought of as seeing religion as an entirely conservative ideology – a set of ruling-class ideas that legitimate class inequalities.

However, Marxists recognise that ideas, including religious ideas, can have *relative autonomy* – they can be partly independent of the capitalist economic base of society.

Thus religion can have a *dual character*, sometimes being a force for change as well as stability.

Ernst Bloch: the principle of hope

▶ The Marxist Bloch (1959) sees religion as having a dual character. He accepts that religion often inhibits change, but argues that it can also inspire protest and rebellion. Religion is an expression of 'the principle of hope' – our dreams of a better life, containing images of utopia.

▶ Images of utopia can sometimes deceive people – e.g. promises of rewards in heaven – but they may also help people to create a vision of a better world and strive for social change.

Liberation Theology (LT)

▶ For centuries the Catholic Church in Latin America had been a very conservative institution encouraging acceptance of poverty and supporting wealthy elites.

▶ LT is a movement that emerged within the Catholic Church in Latin America in the 1960s, with a strong commitment to the poor and opposition to the military dictatorships that then ruled most of the continent.

▶ LT emerged because of the growth of rural poverty and urban slums throughout Latin America, and human rights abuses following military take-overs.

▶ LT emphasises 'praxis' – practical action guided by theory; e.g. priests leading literacy programmes and raising political awareness. Some priests actively resisted state terror.

▶ However, in the 1980s the Church's official attitude changed, the conservative Pope John Paul II condemning LT as being akin to Marxism.

▶ However, LT played an important part in resisting dictatorship and bringing about democracy in Latin America.

Interpretation
The NCR is an example of a religious movement aiming for 'conservative social change' – changing society back to a previous form.

Interpretation
Engels argues that although religion inhibits change by disguising inequality, it can also encourage social change; e.g. lower ranks within the church hierarchy have sometimes supported popular protest.

Analysis
LT shows how the same religious organisation can be both conservative and a force for social change. Both traditional conservative Catholicism and LT based their actions on the same religious texts.

Evaluation
Use LT to criticise traditional Marxist views. Neo-Marxist Maduro (1982) argues that LT shows religion can be a revolutionary force. However, though LT helped bring about democracy, it did not threaten capitalism.

Millenarian movements

Millenarian movements are an example of the desire to change things here and now, to bring about the kingdom of God on earth. Worsley (1968) argues that they expect the total and imminent transformation of this world by supernatural means, creating heaven on earth.

Application

You can link this to the relationship between religion and social change because millenarian movements sometimes developed into secular political movements that overthrew colonial rule in the 1950s and 1960s.

▶ They appeal mainly to the poor because they promise immediate improvement, and they often arise in colonial situations.

▶ European colonialism shattered the traditional tribal social structures and cultures of the colonised peoples.

▶ Worsley studied the *cargo cults* – millenarian movements in Melanesia, where islanders felt deprived when 'cargo' (material goods) arrived in the islands for the colonists.

▶ Cargo cults asserted that the cargo had been meant for the natives but had been diverted by the whites for themselves, and that this was about to be overturned. These movements often led to widespread unrest.

Gramsci: religion and hegemony

Gramsci (1971) is interested in how the ruling class maintain their control over society through ideas rather than simply through coercion (force).

Application

Applied to the relationship between religion and social change, Gramsci sees religion as having a dual character – both a conservative social force and a force for change.

▶ *Hegemony* – ideological domination or leadership of society – is the way the ruling class are able to use ideas such as religion to maintain control; e.g. in Italy in the 1920s/30s, the conservative ideological power of the Catholic Church helped to win support for the fascist regime.

▶ However, in some circumstances religion can challenge the ruling class; e.g. it may help the working class to see through the ruling-class hegemony and some clergy may act as *organic intellectuals* – leaders who can support working-class organisations.

Religion and class conflict

▶ Billings (1990) applies Gramsci's ideas in a case study comparing class struggle in two communities – coalminers and textile workers – in Kentucky in the 1920s and 1930s. Both were working-class and evangelical Protestant, but the miners were much more militant, struggling for better conditions.

Interpretation

Billings shows that the same religion – evangelical Protestantism – can be called upon either to defend the status quo or support and justify the struggle to change it.

▶ The differences in levels of militancy can be understood in terms of hegemony and the role of religion. The miners benefited from the leadership of *organic intellectuals* – miners who were also lay preachers.

ONE TO TRY

Question Assess the view that religious ideas and organisations inevitably act as conservative forces.   (33 marks)

Examiner's Advice Explain the different meanings of 'conservative'. You can then consider evidence to support the view that organisations like the Catholic Church or New Christian Right promote traditional values and/or support the status quo. Include the arguments and evidence of Marxists and feminists on religion defending the interests of privileged groups. You should question whether religion always ('inevitably' in the question) supports the status quo. Refer to the idea of religion having a dual role and use examples of religion acting to create social change (e.g. Weber on Calvinism), but keep a fix on the term 'conservative' and remember this can include change in the form of returning society to traditional values. You can also pick up on the 'ideas *and* organisations' wording in the question and ask whether beliefs may have a dual role while organisations are usually conservative.

---

3 Secularisation

Key Issues

▶ To what extent has a process of secularisation occurred?

▶ What arguments and evidence do sociologists put forward to support secularisation theory?

▶ How has secularisation theory has been applied to the UK and the USA?

▶ Is a spiritual revolution taking place?

Secularisation in Britain

▶ Crockett (1998) estimates that in 1851, 40% or more of the adult population of Britain attended church on Sundays, which led some to claim that the 19th century was a 'golden age' of religiosity.

▶ Wilson (1966) argues that Western societies have been undergoing a long-term process of secularisation, where 'religious beliefs, practices and institutions lose social significance'.

It is certainly the case that there have been some major changes in religion in the UK since the 19th century: a fall in the proportion of the population attending church, an increase in the average age of churchgoers, and greater religious diversity.

Church attendance today

▶ Only 6.3% of the adult population attended church on Sundays in 2005, halving since the 1960s and likely to fall further.

▶ Very few children attend Sunday schools. Church weddings and baptisms are also declining.

▶ The English Church Census (2006) shows attendance at and membership of large religious organisations (e.g. Church of England) have declined – although participation in small religious organisations has increased.

Religious beliefs today

Evidence about religious beliefs from over 60 years of attitude surveys shows that:

▶ More people claim they hold Christian beliefs than actually go to church.

▶ Religious belief is declining, in line with the decline in church attendance and membership.

▶ Gill et al (1998) reviewed almost 100 national surveys on religious belief from 1939 to 1996. This showed a significant decline in belief in a personal god and in traditional teachings about the afterlife.

Religious institutions today

Bruce (2002) agrees with Wilson that all the evidence on secularisation has shown that 'there is a steady and unremitting decline'.

▶ The influence of religion as a social institution is declining. Religion once affected every aspect of life, but now is relegated to the private sphere of individual and family.

▶ The state has taken over many of the functions the church used to perform, e.g. schooling.

▶ The number of clergy fell from 45,000 in 1900 to 34,000 in 2000, while the population increased in size, reducing the church's local, day-to-day influence.

Bruce predicts that the Methodist Church will fold by 2030 and the Church of England will be merely a small voluntary organisation with a large amount of heritage property.

Evaluation
Religion may have declined in Europe but not necessarily in America or elsewhere, so secularisation may not be universal.

Interpretation
Evidence of falling church attendance ignores people who believe but don't go to church.

Interpretation
However, although membership of small religious organisations has grown, this has not made up for the decline of large ones, so the overall trend is still one of decline.

Evaluation
Although there is an increasing number of 'faith schools' in the UK – implying continued religious involvement in education – they are mainly state-funded and must conform to the state's regulations.

Explanations of secularisation

Secularisation and the decline of religion have often been linked to major social changes such as modernisation (the decline of tradition), industrialisation and its effects, and increased social and religious diversity. Sociologists have developed several explanations of secularisation:

1 Rationalisation

Rationalisation is the process by which rational ways of thinking and acting replace religious ones. Max Weber (1905) argues that Western society has undergone a process of rationalisation in the last few centuries.

▶ The 16th century Protestant Reformation undermined the religious worldview of the Middle Ages, replacing it with a modern rational scientific outlook.

▶ The medieval Catholic worldview saw the world as an 'enchanted (or magical) garden' in which God, angels etc. changed the course of events through their supernatural powers and miracle-working interventions.

Disenchantment The Protestant Reformation brought a new worldview that saw God as existing above and outside the world, not as intervening in it. The world had become *disenchanted*, left to run according to the laws of nature.

▶ Events were thus no longer to be explained as the work of unpredictable supernatural beings, but as the predictable workings of natural forces.

▶ Through reason and science, humans could discover the laws of nature, and understand and predict how the world works. Religious explanations of the world are no longer needed.

▶ This enables science to develop, giving humans more power to control nature, further undermining the religious worldview.

A technological worldview Bruce argues that a technological worldview has largely replaced religious explanations of why things happen. Religious worldviews only survive in areas where technology is least effective, e.g. praying for help if you are suffering from an incurable illness.

2 Structural differentiation

Parsons (1951) defines structural differentiation as a process that occurs with industrialisation as many specialised institutions develop to carry out the different functions previously performed by a single institution, such as the church.

▶ Religion dominated pre-industrial society, but with industrialisation it has become a smaller and more specialised institution.

▶ Bruce agrees that religion has become separated from wider society and privatised in the home and family. Religious beliefs are now largely a matter of personal choice, while traditional rituals and symbols have lost meaning.

▶ Even where religion is involved in education or welfare, it must conform to secular controls; e.g. teachers in faith schools must hold qualifications recognised by the state.

▶ Church and state are usually separate in modern society, so the church loses political power.

3 Social and cultural diversity

▶ Wilson argues that in pre-industrial society, local communities shared religious rituals that expressed their shared values, but industrialisation destroys these stable local communities and so destroys religion's base.

▶ Bruce sees industrialisation creating large, impersonal, loose-knit urban centres with diverse beliefs, values and lifestyles. This diversity undermines the believability of religion.

▶ The rise of individualism leads to a decline in community-based religious belief and practice.

Analysis
Explain some of the ways in which the processes of modernisation, industrialisation and diversity might be inter-related.

Analysis
Although scientific explanations do not generally challenge religious beliefs directly, they have greatly reduced the scope for religious explanations.

Application
Explain how structural differentiation means that religion's functions are transferred to other institutions such as the state and it becomes disconnected and disengaged from wider society.

Evaluation
Aldridge points out that a community does not have to be in a particular locality. Religion can be a shared source of identity on a worldwide scale, e.g. Jewish communities. Also, Pentecostal and other groups often flourish in supposedly 'impersonal' urban areas.

4 Religious diversity

Berger (1969) argues that another cause of secularisation is the trend towards religious diversity.

▶ In the Middle Ages, the Catholic Church held an absolute monopoly and had no challengers.

▶ Since the 16th century Protestant Reformation, the number and variety of religious organisations has grown, each with a different version of the truth.

▶ Berger argues that this religious diversity undermines religion's 'plausibility structure' – its believability. Alternative versions of religion enable people to question all of them and this erodes the absolute certainties of traditional religion.

Bruce sees the trend towards religious diversity as the most important cause of secularisation, because it is difficult to live in a world containing a large number of incompatible beliefs without concluding that none of them is wholly true.

5 Cultural defence and cultural transition

Bruce identifies two counter-trends that seem to contradict secularisation theory:

▶ **Cultural defence** Religion provides a focus for the defence of national or ethnic group identity in a struggle against an external force, e.g. Catholicism in Poland before the fall of communism.

▶ **Cultural transition** Religion provides a sense of community for ethnic groups living in a different country and culture.

The spiritual revolution

Some sociologists argue that a 'spiritual revolution' is taking place, with traditional Christianity giving way to a New Age spirituality that emphasises personal development and experience.

▶ The 'spiritual market' is growing, e.g. the huge number of books about self-help and spirituality and the many 'therapies', from meditation to crystal healing.

Heelas and Woodhead studied Kendal to investigate whether traditional religion has declined and how far the growth of spirituality is compensating for this. They distinguish between:

1. **The congregational domain** of traditional and evangelical Christian churches.

2. **The holistic milieu** of spirituality and the New Age.

They found that:

▶ In a typical week in 2000, 7.9% of the population attended church (the congregational domain), and 1.6% took part in spiritual activities (the holistic milieu).

▶ Within the congregational domain, the traditional churches were losing support, while evangelical churches were holding their own. Although fewer people were involved in the holistic milieu, it was growing.

Heelas and Woodhead explain these trends as follows:

1. New Age spirituality has grown because of a massive 'subjective turn' in today's culture – a shift towards exploring your inner self by following a spiritual path.

2. As a result, traditional religions, which demand duty and obedience, are declining.

3. Evangelical churches are more successful than the traditional churches because they emphasise the subjective aspects: spiritual healing and growth through the personal experience of being 'born again'.

4. In the spiritual marketplace, therefore, the winners are those who appeal to personal experience as the only genuine source of meaning and fulfilment, rather than the received teachings and commandments of traditional religion.

Interpretation
It depends how the evidence is interpreted, since opposing views can strengthen a religious group's commitment to its existing beliefs rather than undermining them.

Evaluation
Bruce argues that cultural defence/transition don't contradict secularisation theory, since religion only survives in these situations as a focus for group identity and not as an expression of religious faith; e.g. once communism had fallen in Poland, church attendance declined.

Application
Explain the difference between religion and spirituality. Religion emphasises conforming to church authority, self-sacrifice and deference. Spirituality focuses on personal development, autonomy and connecting to your inner self.

Evaluation
This doesn't mean a spiritual revolution has taken place – the smaller growth of the holistic milieu has not compensated for the larger decline of traditional religion.

Secularisation in the USA

In 1962, Wilson found that 45% of Americans attended church on Sundays, but this was more an expression of the 'American way of life' than of religious beliefs. For Wilson, America is a secular society, because religion there has become superficial.

Bruce (2002) shares Wilson's view. He uses three sources of evidence to support his claim that America is becoming increasingly secular:

1 Declining church attendance

Opinion polls asking people about church attendance suggest it has been stable at about 40% of the population since 1940. However, this figure may well be an exaggeration.

▶ For example, Hadaway et al (1993) found that in one county in Ohio, the attendance level claimed in opinion polls was 83% higher than researchers actually counted going into church.

▶ Evidence suggests that this tendency to exaggerate churchgoing is a recent development.

2 Secularisation from within

Bruce argues that in America, the emphasis on traditional Christian beliefs and glorifying God has declined. Instead, religion has become 'psychologised' – a form of therapy.

▶ American religion has remained popular by becoming less religious – it has become secularised from within. Its purpose has changed from seeking salvation in heaven to seeking personal improvement in this world.

3 Religious diversity and relativism

Bruce identifies *practical relativism* among American Christians – i.e. accepting that others are entitled to hold beliefs different to one's own.

▶ Lynd and Lynd (1929) found in 1924 that 94% of churchgoing young people agreed with the statement 'Christianity is the one true religion'. By 1977 only 41% agreed.

▶ Absolutism has been eroded – we now live in a society where many people hold views that are completely different to ours, undermining our assumption that our own views are absolutely true.

Interpretation

Hadaway shows the problem of simply asking people whether they attend church. The 40% rate of self-reported attendance masks a decline in actual attendance in the USA, because many people who have stopped going will still *say* they attend if asked.

Application

Link Berger's ideas about diversity undermining religion's plausibility structure to this argument.

ONE TO TRY

Read Item A and answer the question that follows.

Item A Some sociologists argue that the secularisation of Western societies has resulted from a process of rationalisation that began in the 16th century with the Protestant Reformation. Weber argued that the Reformation replaced the religious worldview of the Middle Ages with a modern, scientific outlook. Rational ways of thinking and acting replaced religious ones.

Although scientific explanations do not challenge religion directly, they greatly reduce the scope for religious explanations.

Question Using material from **Item A** and elsewhere, assess the view that a process of rationalisation has led to secularisation in Western societies.   (18 marks)

Examiner's Advice Begin by explaining what is meant by both secularisation and rationalisation. The arguments and evidence presented by Weber should be the main focus of your answer. Your assessment should include some of the criticisms made by Tawney and others of Weber's historical analysis and conclusions. You should also discuss alternative explanations of secularisation offered by sociologists including Parsons, Berger, Wilson and Bruce.

4 Religion, Renewal and Choice

Key Issues

▶ Is religion simply changing rather than declining?

▶ Are church attendance statistics a valid measure of religious belief?

▶ Does increased diversity and choice encourage greater involvement in religion or reduce it?

▶ Is secularisation a Eurocentric process?

Postmodernity and religion

Some sociologists reject secularisation theory and argue that religion is simply changing, rather than declining – as a result of changes in wider society, such as greater individualism and consumerism, or a shift from modern to late modern or postmodern society.

Believing without belonging

Grace Davie (2007) argues that religion is not declining but simply taking a different, more *privatised* form.

▶ People no longer go to church because they feel they have to, so although churchgoing has declined, this is because attendance is now a matter of personal choice rather than an obligation.

▶ We now have *believing without belonging* – people hold religious beliefs but don't go to church. Thus, the decline of traditional religion is matched by the growth of a new form of religion.

▶ There is a trend towards 'vicarious religion', where a small number of professional clergy practise religion on behalf of a much larger number of people.

▶ In societies like Britain, despite low attendance, many people still use the church for rites of passage – baptisms, weddings and funerals.

▶ Davie rejects secularisation theory's assumption that modernisation affects every society in the same way. Instead there are *multiple modernities*; e.g. Britain and America are both modern societies, but with very different patterns of religion – high church attendance in America, low in Britain, but accompanied by believing without belonging.

Spiritual shopping

Danielle Hervieu-Léger (2000) supports the theme of personal choice and believing without belonging.

▶ There has been *cultural amnesia* – a loss of collective memory. People have lost the religion that used to be handed down from generation to generation through family and church.

▶ Greater equality has undermined the traditional Church's power to impose religion from above, so young people no longer inherit a fixed religious identity.

▶ However, while traditional institutional religion has declined, religion continues through individual consumerism. People have become *spiritual shoppers*. Religion is now *individualised* – we now develop our own 'do-it-yourself' beliefs.

Evaluation

The British Social Attitudes surveys from 1983 to 2000 show that both church attendance *and* belief in God are declining. If Davie were right, we would expect to see higher levels of belief.

Interpretation

If people are not willing to attend church regularly, this may just reflect the declining strength of their beliefs rather than some continuing religiosity.

Interpretation

Hervieu-Léger's views can be related to the idea of *late modernity* – the idea that in recent times some of the trends found in modern society have begun to accelerate, e.g. the decline of tradition and increasing individualism.

Hervieu-Léger argues that two new religious types are emerging:

▶ **Pilgrims** follow an individual path in a search for self-discovery, e.g. New Age or through individual 'therapy'.

▶ **Converts** join religious groups that offer a strong sense of belonging. This re-creates a sense of community, e.g. evangelical movements and ethnic minority churches.

Lyon: 'Jesus in Disneyland'

Lyon (2000) argues that postmodern society has several features that are changing the nature of religion – globalisation, the increased importance of the media and consumerism. As a result, traditional religion is giving way to new religious forms and these demonstrate its continuing strength.

Interpretation
Lyon's explanation comes from a postmodernist approach. He rejects secularisation theory as a meta-narrative – i.e. merely someone's 'big story' about how things are supposed to be.

The relocation of religion As a result of globalisation, there is increased movement of religious ideas across national boundaries.

▶ The media now saturate us with images and messages from around the globe, giving us instant access to the ideas and beliefs of previously remote religions.

▶ These ideas are 'disembedded' as the media lift them out of their local contexts and move them to a different place and time; e.g. televangelism relocates religion to the internet and TV, allowing believers to express their faith without attending church.

▶ So religion becomes de-institutionalised – its signs and images become detached from their place in religious institutions, floating and multiplying on TV and in cyber-space, a cultural resource that individuals can adapt for their own purposes.

Evaluation
Bruce argues that this consumerist religion is weak religion – it has little effect on the lives of its adherents. As such, he sees its rise as evidence of secularisation, not of the continuing vitality of religion.

Religious consumerism Postmodern society involves the idea that we now construct our identities through what we consume.

▶ This is also true of religion: we are 'spiritual shoppers', choosing religious beliefs and practices to meet our individual needs, from the vast range on offer in the religious marketplace.

▶ We can pick and mix elements of different faiths to suit our tastes and make them part of our identity.

▶ In Lyon's view, religion has relocated to the *sphere of consumption*. People may have ceased to belong to religious organisations, but have not abandoned religion. They have become 'religious consumers', making conscious choices about which elements of religion they find useful.

One effect of having access to a great variety of different beliefs is loss of faith in 'meta-narratives' (worldviews that claim to have the absolute, authoritative truth, such as the traditional religions) because people become sceptical that any one of them is really true.

Application
Lyon's view is a criticism of secularisation theory for assuming that religion is declining and being replaced by a 'disenchanted' rational, scientific worldview.

Previously dominant organisations and traditions thus lose their authority and decline. In their place, many new movements spring up that consumers can 'sample'.

Re-enchantment of the world Lyon sees recent decades as a period of *re-enchantment*, with the growth of unconventional beliefs and practices.

▶ Although traditional religion has declined in Europe, Lyon points to the growth of non-traditional religion in the West and elsewhere.

Religious market theory

Evaluation
Religious market theory is a critique of secularisation theory, which they see as eurocentric and failing to explain religion's continuing vitality in America and elsewhere.

Stark and Bainbridge (1985) advocate religious market theory (also called rational choice theory). They criticise secularisation theory for its 'distorted view' of the past and future: there was no past 'golden age' of religion, nor is it likely that everyone will be an atheist in the future.

Stark and Bainbridge base religious market theory on two assumptions:

1. People are naturally religious and religion meets human needs.

2. People make rational choices based on the costs and benefits of the available religious options.

▶ Religion is attractive because it provides us with supernatural *compensators* when real rewards are unobtainable; e.g. immortality is unobtainable, but religion compensates by promising life after death.

▶ Only religion can provide such compensators, because only it can promise supernatural rewards.

Historical cycle Stark and Bainbridge suggest there is a historical cycle of religious decline, revival and renewal: as established churches decline, they leave a gap in the market for new sects and cults.

Competition Religious market theorists argue that competition leads to improvements in the quality of the religious 'goods' on offer. Churches that make their product attractive will succeed in attracting more 'customers'.

America versus Europe

Demand for religion increases when there is a choice, because consumers can find one that meets their needs. In the USA, religion is strong because a healthy market exists where religions grow or decline according to consumer demand. But where there is a religious monopoly, as in most European countries (e.g. the Church of England), lack of choice has led to decline.

Interpretation
From this point of view, secularisation theory is one-sided: it sees the decline, but ignores the growth of new religions and religious revivals.

Evaluation
Norris and Inglehart (2004) show that high levels of religious participation exist in Catholic countries where the Church has a near monopoly, e.g. Venezuela. This contradicts Stark and Bainbridge's theory.

Existential security theory

Norris and Inglehart (2004) reject religious market theory on the grounds that it only applies to America and fails to explain the variations in religiosity between societies.

They argue that the reason for such variations is not different degrees of religious choice, but different degrees of *existential security* – 'the feeling that survival is secure enough that it can be taken for granted'.

▶ Religion meets a need for security, and so groups and societies where people feel insecure have a high level of demand for religion. These tend to be low-income groups and societies.

▶ This explains why poor Third World countries – and poor people in rich countries – remain religious, while people in prosperous Western countries are more secure and have become more secular.

Europe *vs.* America

▶ Western Europe is becoming more secular because these societies are relatively equal and secure, with well developed welfare states which reduce insecurity among the poor, whereas the USA remains religious.

▶ Similarly, Gill and Lundegaarde (2004) argue that the more a country spends on welfare, the lower its level of religious participation.

Evaluation
Norris and Inglehart only see religion as a negative response to deprivation. They ignore the positive reasons people have for religious participation.

Analysis
This is because America is also the most unequal of the rich societies, with high levels of poverty and a weak welfare system.

ONE TO TRY

Question Assess the view that religion is not in decline but simply changing as a result of changes in wider society. (33 marks)

Examiner's Advice Start with a brief explanation of secularisation – the idea that religion is in decline. You should then focus on the changes in society that may have led to religion changing but not declining. These include individualism, consumerism, greater equality, a decline in communities and the move towards postmodern society. Link these to possible changes in the nature of religious beliefs and practices – e.g. privatised religion, 'spiritual shopping' and religious consumerism. Use theories such as Hervieu-Léger, Stark and Bainbridge, and Lyon. Evaluate by criticising their claims and/or by considering evidence presented by secularisation theorists, but don't turn your answer into a standard 'secularisation' response – keep focused on 'change not decline'.

5 Religion in a global context

Key Issues

▶ What is religion's role in economic development in a global context?

▶ How can we explain the nature of religious fundamentalism?

▶ What is religion's role in international conflict?

Religion and development

▶ According to secularisation theory, development undermines religion: modern science and technology destroy belief in the supernatural.

▶ However, religion may also contribute to development, e.g. Weber's claim that the Protestant ethic helped bring about modern capitalism.

▶ More recently, sociologists have examined the role religion plays in development in today's globalising world.

God and globalisation in India

Globalisation has brought rapid economic growth in India and rising prosperity to a new middle class. Nanda (2008) examines the role of Hinduism, the religion of 85% of the population, in legitimating the rise of a new Hindu 'ultra-nationalism' and the prosperity of the Indian middle class.

Hinduism and consumerism

Interpretation
Poverty and existential insecurity cannot explain this increased religiosity because the middle class are not poor.

According to secularisation theory, the prosperous, scientifically educated, urban middle class are precisely the people who will be the first to adopt a secular worldview. Yet surveys show that Indians are becoming *more* religious and that urban, educated Indians are more religious than rural, less literate Indians.

Nanda argues that this increasing religiosity is the result of the middle class's ambivalence about their newfound wealth, stemming from a tension between their new prosperity and the traditional Hindu belief in renouncing materialism.

▶ This is resolved by the modern holy men and tele-gurus who preach the message that desire is not bad, but a manifestation of divinity that motivates people to do things.

▶ These business-friendly versions of Hinduism legitimate the position of the middle class and allow them to adjust to globalised consumer capitalism.

Application
In this Hindu ultra-nationalism, the worship of Hindu gods has become the same as worshipping the nation of India: Hinduism has become a *civil religion*.

▶ Hinduism also legitimates a triumphalist version of Indian nationalism. Politicians and the media constantly promote the view that India's success in the global market is due to the superiority of 'Hindu values'.

▶ Hinduism has also penetrated public life and the supposedly secular state; e.g. 'Hindu sciences' such as astrology are being taught as academic subjects in public universities and being used supposedly to predict natural disasters.

Pentecostalism in Latin America

Berger (2003) argues that Pentecostalism in Latin America acts as a 'functional equivalent' to Weber's Protestant ethic, encouraging the development of capitalism in the same way as Calvinism did in 16th century Europe.

▶ Like Calvinism, Pentecostalism demands an ascetic (self-denying) way of life emphasising personal discipline and hard work. This encourages its members to prosper and become upwardly mobile.

▶ For Berger, something like Protestantism is necessary to promote economic development and raise a society out of poverty. This can be led by an active minority with an ethic of this-worldly asceticism, such as the Pentecostalists.

Pentecostalism: global and local

▶ In the last five centuries, Christianity has globalised itself by expanding into South America and Africa. Lehmann (2002) suggests the first phase of this was through colonisation, with Christianity being imposed on the indigenous populations by conquest.

▶ In the second phase, over the last century, it has spread because it gained a popular following from below, mainly through Pentecostalist and similar charismatic movements.

▶ Pentecostalism creates new local religious forms, incorporating existing local beliefs (e.g. spirit possession), rather than replacing them with ones imposed from outside.

▶ In Africa, this has led to the 'Africanisation' of Christianity rather than the total disappearance of indigenous religions.

> **Analysis**
> Pentecostalism has also succeeded in the developing countries because it appeals particularly to the poor who make up the vast majority of the population.

Religious fundamentalism

In a global context, the issue of religious fundamentalism has emerged as a major area of concern, notably in relation to international Islamist terrorism.

Fundamentalism and cosmopolitanism

Giddens (1990; 1991; 1999) defines fundamentalists as traditionalists who wish to return to the fundamentals of their faith and who have an unquestioning belief in the literal truth of scripture.

▶ They believe that they alone possess the truth and are intolerant of other views.

▶ They rely upon the guardians of tradition, e.g. clergy, to interpret the sacred text and lay down rules that determine their lifestyle.

▶ However, while fundamentalists detest modernity, they use modern methods to express and spread their beliefs, e.g. the internet, e-mail, televangelism and the 'electronic church'.

▶ Giddens sees fundamentalism as a reaction to globalisation, which undermines traditional norms, e.g. about gender and sexuality. He contrasts it with cosmopolitanism – a way of thinking that embraces modernity, is tolerant, open and constantly reflects on and modifies beliefs ('reflexive' thinking).

▶ Cosmopolitanism sees lifestyle as a personal choice, not something dictated by an external religious authority. It emphasises the pursuit of personal meaning and self-improvement rather than submission to authority.

> **Evaluation**
> Giddens' description of fundamentalism as a defensive reaction to modernity ignores the fact that *reinventing* tradition is also a modern, 'reflexive' activity.

> **Application**
> Reflexive thinking requires people to justify their views by the use of rational arguments and evidence rather than simply by appealing to sacred texts or tradition.

Monotheism and fundamentalism

Bruce (2007) sees the main cause of fundamentalism as the perception by religious traditionalists that globalisation threatens their beliefs and lifestyle. This leads them to develop rigid rules about belief and behaviour.

However, Bruce regards fundamentalism as being confined to monotheistic religions (Judaism, Islam, Christianity). Polytheistic religions (e.g. Hinduism) that believe in many gods are unlikely to produce fundamentalism.

Two fundamentalisms

Bruce argues that while fundamentalists share the same characteristics such as belief in the literal truth of the sacred text, different fundamentalist movements have different origins.

▶ **In the West**, fundamentalism is usually a reaction to change *within society*, e.g. trends towards diversity and choice. So the New Christian Right in America has developed in opposition to family diversity, sexual 'permissiveness', gender equality and secular education.

▶ **In the Third World**, fundamentalism is usually a reaction to changes being thrust on a society from *outside*, e.g. 'Western' values imposed by foreign capitalism. Here, fundamentalism involves resistance to the state's attempts to reduce the social influence of religion.

> **Analysis**
> Bruce argues this is because monotheistic religions are based on a notion of God's will as revealed through a single, authoritative sacred text. Polytheists lack a single all-powerful deity and a single authoritative text, leaving much more scope for differing interpretations.

Cultural defence

Bruce (2002) sees one function of religion as cultural defence – religion unites a community against an external threat and this often gives it a prominent role in politics. Religion has special significance for its followers because it symbolises the group or society's collective identity.

Poland From 1945 to 1989, Poland was under communist rule imposed from outside by the Soviet Union. Although the Catholic Church did not always challenge the communist regime openly, it served as a popular rallying point for opposition, e.g. actively supporting the Solidarity free trade union movement that contributed to the fall of communism.

Iran Western capitalist powers and oil companies had long had influence in Iran, installing a pro-Western regime headed by the Shah. During the 1960s and 70s, his successor embarked on a policy of rapid modernisation and Westernisation. Islam became the focus for resistance to change and to the Shah. The 1979 revolution brought the creation of the Islamic Republic, in which clergy held state power and were able to impose Islamic Shari'a law.

Application
Use these two examples to show that religion can be used to defend national identity against domination by an external power. In both cases, the role of religion has to be understood in a *transnational* context.

The 'clash of civilisations'

Religion has been at the centre of a number of recent global conflicts, e.g. the '9/11' Islamist attacks in the USA.

▶ Huntington (1993), an American neo-conservative, claims these conflicts have intensified since the collapse of communism in 1989 and are symptoms of a wider 'clash of civilisations'.

▶ He identifies seven civilisations: Western, Latin American, Confucian (China), Japanese, Islamic, Hindu and Slavic-Orthodox.

▶ Each civilisation has a common cultural background and is closely identified with one of the world's great religions.

▶ Since the fall of communism, religious differences have become a major source of identity. Globalisation also makes nation-states less important as a source of identity and makes contact between civilisations easier, increasing the likelihood of old conflicts re-emerging.

▶ Religious differences are creating a new set of hostile 'us and them' relationships, with increased competition between civilisations for economic and military power.

Huntington sees history as a struggle of 'progress against barbarism' and predicts growing conflict between 'the West and the rest'.

Evaluation
Jackson (2006) sees Huntington's work as an example of *orientalism* – a western ideology that stereotypes Eastern nations and people (especially Muslims) as untrustworthy, inferior or fanatical 'Others'.

The real clash of civilisations?

▶ World Values Survey data indicates that the issue dividing the West from the Muslim world is not democracy but sexuality. Support for democracy is high in both the West and the Muslim world, but there are great differences in attitudes to divorce, abortion, gender equality and gay rights.

▶ While Western attitudes have become more liberal, in the Muslim world they remain traditional.

Interpretation
Inglehart and Norris argue that there is no global agreement about *self-expression values*, such as gender equality and freedom of speech. It is these values that constitute the real 'clash of civilisations' between Muslim societies and the West.

ONE TO TRY

Question Assess sociological explanations of the rise of religious fundamentalism.
(33 marks)

Examiner's Advice You need to assess a range of explanations, including those offered by Giddens, Bruce, Bauman and Castells. Start by giving a brief definition of fundamentalism, indicating its possible forms and suggesting why it has been the focus of recent sociological interest. Link the rise of fundamentalism to cultural defence theory and to Huntington's 'clash of civilisations' claim. Evaluation could take the form of criticisms of each of the different explanations as you consider each in turn and in a final evaluation paragraph.

6 Organisations, movements and members

Key Issues

▶ What are the key characteristics of the main types of religious organisation?

▶ How can we explain the development of different types of organisations and movements?

▶ Why and how does religious participation vary by class, ethnicity, gender and age?

Types of religious organisation

Sociologists are interested in the different types of religious organisation, their development and membership.

Church and sect

Troeltsch distinguished between two main types of organisation – church and sect.

1. *Churches* are large, with millions of members, place few demands on members, have a bureaucratic hierarchy, claim a monopoly of truth and are universalistic, ideologically conservative and linked to the state.

2. *Sects* are small, exclusive groups demanding real commitment from members, are hostile to wider society, recruit from the poor and oppressed, often have charismatic leadership and believe they have a monopoly of religious truth.

Denomination and cult

▶ Niebuhr (1929) identifies *denominations* (e.g. Methodism) as midway between churches and sects. Membership is less exclusive, they broadly accept society's values, are not linked to the state and impose some minor restrictions, but are not as demanding as sects and are tolerant of other religions.

▶ *Cults* are the least organised of all religious organisations. They are highly individualistic, small, loose-knit groupings without a sharply defined belief system. Many are world-affirming.

New religious movements (NRMs)

Since the 1960s, there has been a big increase in NRMs, e.g. the Moonies; Scientology. Wallis (1984) categorises NRMs into three groups based on their relationship to the outside world:

1. **World-rejecting NRMs** (e.g. Moonies; Branch Davidian; the People's Temple) have a clear notion of God, are highly critical of the outside world and expect radical change. Members must break with their former life, live communally and have restricted contact with the outside world. The movement controls all aspects of their lives.

2. **World-accommodating NRMs** (e.g. neo-Pentecostalists; Subud) are often breakaways from existing churches. They neither accept nor reject the world, focusing on religious rather than worldly matters. Members tend to lead conventional lives.

3. **World-affirming NRMs** (e.g. Scientology; TM; Human Potential) often lack some of the conventional features of religion. They offer followers access to spiritual or supernatural powers and accept the world as it is, promising followers success in their goals. Followers are often customers rather than members.

Evaluation
Criticise these descriptions of religious organisations by pointing out they do not fit today's reality; e.g. some churches have lost their monopoly and been reduced to the status of denominations.

Analysis
Explain differences and similarities between religious organisations by asking how they see themselves and how they are seen by wider society.

Evaluation
Wallis's typology ignores the diversity of beliefs that may exist *within* a NRM.

Analysis
These are world-affirming because they claim to offer special knowledge that enables followers to unlock their own spiritual powers – they are psychologising religions.

Sects and cults

Stark and Bainbridge (1985) argue that just one criterion is needed to distinguish between religious organisations – the degree of tension between the group and wider society. Two kinds of organisation are in conflict with wider society – sects and cults:

▶ **Sects** result from splits in existing organisations breaking away and offering *other-worldly benefits* to those suffering economic or ethical deprivation.

▶ **Cults** are new religions (e.g. Scientology) or ones that have been imported (e.g. TM). They offer *this-worldly benefits* to individuals suffering psychic or health deprivation.

Stark and Bainbridge subdivide cults according to how organised they are.

▶ **Audience cults** – the least organised, with no formal membership and little interaction between members.

▶ **Client cults** – a consultant/client relationship, with 'therapies' promising personal fulfilment.

▶ **Cultic movements** – more organised, exclusivist, requiring high levels of commitment, claiming to meet all their members' religious needs.

> **Evaluation**
> Assess these claims by pointing out that some of the examples Stark and Bainbridge use do not fit neatly into any one of their categories.

Explaining the growth of religious movements

Several explanations have been offered for the rapid growth of sects and cults since the 1960s.

1 Marginality

Weber (1922) argued that sects appeal to disprivileged groups who are marginal to society.

▶ Sects offer a solution to their lack of status by offering their members a *theodicy of disprivilege* – a religious explanation of their disadvantage.

▶ Many sects and millenarian movements have recruited from the marginalised poor.

> **Application**
> Use examples such as the Christian belief that 'the meek shall inherit the earth' to show the appeal religion may have to disprivileged groups.

2 Relative deprivation

It is possible for someone who is quite privileged nevertheless to *feel* deprived compared with others; e.g. some middle-class people may feel spiritually deprived.

▶ People may then turn to sects for a sense of community.

▶ Stark and Bainbridge argue that it is the relatively deprived who break away from churches to form sects.

> **Evaluation**
> Relative deprivation offers an alternative explanation to marginality. E.g. the Moonies have recruited mainly from educated middle-class whites.

3 Social change and NRMs

Wilson (1970) argues that periods of rapid change undermine established norms, producing *anomie* (normlessness). Those most affected may turn to sects, e.g. Methodism during the industrial revolution. Social change may also stimulate the growth of NRMs today:

▶ **World-rejecting NRMs** (WRNRMs) Social changes from the 1960s gave young people freedom, enabling an idealistic counter-culture to develop, while the growth of radical political movements offered alternative ideas about the future. WRNRMs were attractive because they offered a more idealistic way of life.

▶ **World-affirming NRMs** (WANRMs) have grown in response to modernity. Modernity brings the rationalisation of work, which ceases to be a source of identity, and the need to achieve. WANRMs provide both a sense of identity and techniques promising worldly success.

The dynamics of sects and NRMs

How do sects and NRMs change over their 'lifetime'?

Denomination or death Niebuhr (1929) argues that sects are world-rejecting organisations that come into existence by splitting from an established church. Within a generation, they either die out or compromise with the world, abandoning their extreme ideas to become a denomination.

> **Analysis**
> There may be several reasons for this: second generation members lack commitment, ascetic sects become prosperous and compromise with the world, or the leader's death may cause the sect to collapse.

The sectarian cycle Stark and Bainbridge (1985) see religious organisations moving through a cycle: *schism* (splitting from a church); *initial fervour* and charismatic leadership; *denominationalism* and cooling of fervour; *establishment*, as the sect becomes world-accepting; *further schism*.

Established sects Wilson (1966) argues that not all sects follow this pattern – it depends on how the sect answers the question, 'What shall we do to be saved?'

▶ **Conversionist sects**, whose aim is to convert large numbers of people, are likely to grow rapidly into larger denominations.

▶ **Adventist sects** keep themselves separate from the corrupt world, which prevents them from compromising and becoming a denomination.

▶ **Established sects** Some sects survive for many generations, e.g. Amish and Mormons.

The growth of the New Age

Heelas (2008) estimates that audience or client cults in the UK cover about 2,000 activities and 146,000 practitioners. They are extremely diverse, including belief in UFOs, astrology, crystals, alternative medicine, yoga, meditation etc. Heelas (1996) suggests two common themes among the New Age:

▶ **Self-spirituality** New Agers seeking the spiritual have turned away from traditional 'external' churches and instead look inside themselves to find it.

▶ **De-traditionalisation** The New Age rejects the spiritual authority of external traditional sources such as priests and instead values personal experience.

Postmodernity and the New Age

Drane (1999) argues that New Age appeal is part of a shift towards postmodern society. People have lost faith in experts (e.g. scientists) and are disillusioned with the churches' failure to meet their spiritual needs.

The New Age and modernity Bruce (1995) argues that the growth of the New Age is a feature of the latest phase of *modern* society, not postmodernity.

▶ Modern society values individualism (a key principle of New Age beliefs), which is also an important value among those in the 'expressive professions' concerned with human potential, e.g. social workers, artists.

▶ New Age eclecticism ('pick and mix spiritual shopping') is typical of late modern society, reflecting consumerism.

Heelas (1996) sees the New Age and modernity as linked in four ways:

▶ **A source of identity** In modern society, the individual has a fragmented identity. New Age beliefs offer a source of 'authentic' identity.

▶ **Consumer culture** creates dissatisfaction. The New Age offers an alternative way to achieve perfection.

▶ **Rapid social change** in modern society creates anomie. The New Age provides a sense of certainty and truth.

▶ **Decline of organised religion** leaves the way open to the New Age as an alternative.

Religiosity and social groups

As we have seen, different *social classes* tend to be attracted to different beliefs and organisations – e.g. lower classes and world-rejecting sects. However, ethnicity, gender and age are also important.

Gender and religiosity

▶ More women than men believe in God, sin etc and participate in religious activities. In 2005, 1.8 million women were churchgoers as against 1.36 million men.

Application
This gender pattern seems at odds with feminist claims about the patriarchal attitudes of most religions.

▷ Bruce (1996) estimates twice as many women as men are involved in sects. Heelas and Woodhead (2005) found 80% of the holistic milieu in Kendal were female.

Socialisation and gender role Miller and Hoffman argue women are more religious because they are socialised to be more passive, obedient and caring – qualities valued by most religions.

▷ Davie (1994) argues that women's closer proximity to birth and death brings them closer to 'ultimate' questions about life that religion is concerned with.

Women and the New Age As women are more often associated with a healing role, they may be more attracted than men to New Age movements.

▷ Bruce argues child-rearing makes women less aggressive and more cooperative and caring – fitting the expressive emphasis of the New Age.

▷ Brown (2001) argues that New Age religions appeal to women's wish for autonomy.

Compensation for deprivation Glock and Stark argue that deprivation is more common among women. This explains their higher level of sect membership:

Analysis
Explain this link by identifying aspects of New Age movements that involve healing or 'the natural' and that may thus appeal to women.

▷ **Organismic deprivation** Women are more likely to suffer ill health and seek healing.

▷ **Ethical deprivation** Women are more morally conservative and thus attracted to the conservatism of some sects.

▷ **Social deprivation** Women are more likely to be poor and therefore join sects.

Ethnicity and religiosity

There are higher than average rates for most minority groups. Muslims, Hindus and black Christians are more likely to see religion as important. There are several possible reasons:

Evaluation
Despite minorities' higher participation rates, there has been some decline in the importance of religion for all ethnic groups, especially among the second generation.

▷ **Country of origin** Most minorities originate from countries with higher levels of religious practice and they maintain this pattern in the UK.

▷ **Cultural defence** Religion offers a cultural identity in a hostile environment, a means of preserving one's culture and coping with oppression in a racist society.

▷ **Cultural transition** Religion is a means of easing the transition into a new culture by providing support and community for minority groups in their new environment. But once a group has made the transition into the wider society, religion may lose its role.

Age and religious participation

The general pattern of participation is that the older a person is, the more likely they are to attend religious services – with two exceptions, the under 15s and the over 65s.

▷ **Under 15s** are more likely to go to church because they may be made to attend by parents.

▷ **Over 65s** are more likely to be sick or disabled and unable to attend.

Interpretation
Link the idea that each generation is less religious than their parents to secularisation theory.

▷ **The ageing effect** People turn to religion as they get older. As they approach death, they become more concerned about the afterlife.

▷ **The generational effect** Religion becomes less popular with each new generation. Churches are full of older people because they grew up when religion was more popular.

Question Assess sociological explanations of the development of non-traditional forms of religious organisation such as new religious movements, sects and cults.
(33 marks)

ONE TO TRY

Examiner's Advice You should start by describing the range of 'non-traditional' organisations. You should look at different typologies and definitions of religious organisations here, such as Troeltsch, Niebuhr, Wallis, Stark and Bainbridge. You need to examine a range of sociological explanations including Weber, relative deprivation, the impact of social change, modernity and postmodernity. You should evaluate each theory as you explain it as well as in your final conclusion.

7 Ideology and science

Key Issues
▶ What is the difference between open and closed belief systems?
▶ What are the different views of science as a belief system?
▶ What is ideology and what do sociologists see as its role?

Science as a belief system

Science and technology have had an enormous impact on society over the last few centuries, undermining religion and leading to a widespread 'faith in science'. The key feature of science is its *cognitive power*: science enables us to explain, predict and control the world.

Science as an open belief system

Popper (1959) claims science is an 'open' belief system, open to criticism and testing.

▶ Science is based on the principle of *falsificationism*: scientists try to falsify existing theories by seeking evidence to disprove them. If evidence contradicts a theory, the theory is discarded and a better one sought. In this way, knowledge grows.

▶ However, scientific knowledge is not absolute truth. It can always be tested and potentially falsified.

The CUDOS norms Merton (1973) argues that science as an organised social activity has a set of norms ('CUDOS') that promote the growth of knowledge by encouraging openness:

▶ *C*ommunism Knowledge must be shared with the scientific community.

▶ *U*niversalism Scientific knowledge is judged by universal, objective criteria (testing).

▶ *D*isinterestedness Seeking knowledge for its own sake.

▶ *O*rganised *S*cepticism Every theory is open to criticism and testing.

Closed belief systems

Horton (1970) distinguishes between open and closed belief systems. Like Popper, he sees science as an open belief system. However, religion is a closed belief system: it makes knowledge-claims that cannot be overturned.

▶ A closed belief system has 'get-out clauses' that prevent it from being disproved in the eyes of its believers.

▶ Polanyi (1958) argues that belief systems have three devices to sustain themselves in the face of contradictory evidence: circularity; subsidiary explanations and denying legitimacy to rival beliefs.

Science as a closed system

Scientific paradigms Kuhn (1970) argues that a science such as physics is based on a *paradigm* (set of shared assumptions).

▶ This tells scientists what reality is like, defining problems, methods, equipment and even likely research findings.

▶ Most of the time, scientists are engaged in *normal science* within the paradigm.

▶ Scientists who challenge the paradigm are likely to be ridiculed – except during periods of *scientific revolution*, when accumulated evidence undermines it.

The sociology of scientific knowledge

Interpretivists argue that scientific knowledge is socially constructed.

Evaluation
Science may cause problems as well as solve them, through 'manufactured risks' – e.g. pollution, global warming and weapons of mass destruction.

Evaluation
Some argue that science is a self-sustaining, closed belief system. Polanyi argues that *all* belief systems reject fundamental challenges to their knowledge-claims – science is no different.

Application
A scientific paradigm can be seen as a form of closed belief system; e.g. scientific education and training socialises new scientists into faith in the paradigm.

Interpretation
Interpretivist claims point to science as not being objective: rather than discovering objective truths, science is created by social groups.

▶ Knorr-Cetina (1999) argues that what scientists study in the laboratory is highly 'constructed' and far removed from the 'natural' world they are supposedly studying.

▶ Woolgar (1988) argues that scientists have to persuade the scientific community to accept their interpretations of the world. A scientific fact is simply a shared, socially constructed belief.

Marxism, feminism and postmodernism

Marxism and feminism see science as serving the interests of dominant groups – the ruling class or men respectively. Many scientific developments are driven by capitalism's need for knowledge to make profit. Postmodernists also reject science's claims to have 'the truth'. Some argue that science has become *technoscience*, serving capitalist interests by producing commodities for profit.

Analysis
Explain how this fits postmodernist theory. Lyotard (1984) argues that science is a *meta-narrative* – it is just one more 'discourse' that is used to dominate people.

Ideology

'Ideology' refers to a belief system, worldview or set of ideas. The term often includes negative aspects, e.g. beliefs that are false or offer a partial/biased view of reality; conceal the interests of a group or legitimate (justify) inequalities; prevent change by misleading people about their situation; are irrational and closed to criticism.

Interpretation
When someone uses the term ideology to describe a belief system, it often means they regard it as factually and/or morally wrong.

Marxism and ideology

Marxism sees society as divided into two opposed classes: a capitalist ruling class and a working class forced to sell their labour.

▶ The capitalist class exploit workers' labour to produce profit.

▶ It is in the workers' interests to overthrow capitalism by revolution and create a classless communist society. However, revolution cannot occur until the working class become aware of the reality of their exploitation – *class consciousness*.

▶ Ruling-class ideology or hegemony (ideological leadership of society) prevents class consciousness developing by legitimating capitalism.

▶ However, Gramsci (1971) believes that ultimately the working class will overthrow capitalism, led by a party of class-conscious 'organic intellectuals'.

Evaluation
It may not be ideology that prevents attempts to overthrow capitalism, but economic factors (e.g. fear of unemployment) that keep workers from rebelling.

Feminism and ideology

Feminists see gender inequality as legitimated by *patriarchal ideology*.

▶ Religious beliefs and practices often define women as inferior; e.g. menstruating women regarded as unclean and excluded from rituals.

Evaluation
Not all religious belief systems subordinate women; e.g. before the monotheistic patriarchal religions, matriarchal religions with female deities were common.

ONE TO TRY

Read Item A and answer the question that follows.

Item A According to Marxists, capitalist society is divided into a minority capitalist ruling class and an exploited majority. Although it is in the workers' interests to replace capitalism, attempts to overthrow it are rare. For Marxists, this is because the ruling class control the production of ideas, producing ideology that prevents the working class from seeing their true position. Feminists take a similar view, but they see the dominant ideology as subordinating women.

Question Using material from **Item A** and elsewhere, assess the claim that institutions such as religion produce ruling-class ideology that legitimates the status quo.

(18 marks)

Examiner's Advice Begin by explaining what is meant by ruling-class ideology. Arguments and evidence presented by Marxists should be your main focus, including Gramsci's views about hegemony. Your assessment should include criticisms made of Marxist claims. Use material from Item A, e.g. to consider feminist ideas. You could also refer to alternative views of religious ideas, e.g. feminist, functionalist.

Practice question and student answer

Question

'Despite its claim to be the glue that holds society together, religion is more likely to be the cause of division.'

Assess this view in the light of sociological arguments and evidence. (33 marks)

Student answer by Brenda

Some sociologists – in particular, functionalists – claim that religion performs a vital role in society. Religion holds society together by offering a set of norms and values that people can live their lives by. Other sociologists, however, argue that this is an illusion and that religion is more often a source of division in society.

Functionalists have made a strong case for religion acting in a positive manner. Durkheim saw religion as providing the 'social cement' necessary if society was to survive. It creates stability, identity and a 'collective conscience'. When individuals share in the same religious rituals, ceremonies and beliefs, it creates unity in the social group. This also offers individuals an identity tied into that of the social group. The group shares the same set of common values that Durkheim saw as moral bonds through which individuals understand what is appropriate behaviour.

Other functionalists agree with Durkheim. Parsons puts religious values at the heart of the 'central value system' that he claims is at the core of society. To Parsons, religion has a major role to play in socialisation. Religion also helps people deal with the psychological pressures of life. For example, Malinowski observed the Trobriand islanders who lived partly from fishing. He noted that they have more religious rituals when fishing outside the safety of the lagoon. Ocean fishing is much more dangerous and uncertain, so it is always accompanied by 'canoe magic' which gives people a feeling they have some control over events.

Many other examples show the power that religion has to bind people together. Sects may also be so tightly bound together that they will commit mass suicide. Islamic fundamentalists have altered the whole social structure in countries like Iran.

However, some sociologists suggest that functionalist theory might have underestimated the possible negative aspects of religion. It may be that functionalist views of the role of religion are more correct about small-scale, traditional society than large-scale industrial societies.

Some sociologists go further and argue that religion represents one of the major areas of conflict in the modern world. Huntington argues that there is a 'clash of civilisations'. He thinks that Western civilisation, which is mainly Christian, is under threat from Islam, which he believes is seeking to remove other faiths and become the dominant world faith. He claims this is the major conflict that will dominate the world over the coming years.

This introduction isn't much more than a re-statement of the question. It would be better to question the question – e.g. could religion be both 'social glue' in some cases and a cause of division in others?

A good summary of Durkheim's views. Brenda maintains a focus on the issue of how religion may act as a force holding society together.

Brenda touches on Parsons but needs to say more and link it to the question. Her account of canoe magic is accurate, but she needs to go on to make the relevant point from it about whether and how religion acts as a social 'glue'.

These examples need some links to the question.

A useful evaluative point that implies that the claim in the question may be true in some contexts, but not necessarily all.

Good to use a more contemporary theory such as Huntington's. While you need the 'classical' theories such as Durkheim's in essays, it's important to use recent ones, too.

This is quite a good paragraph, although it lacks a full explanation of the Marxist theory of religion and relies instead primarily on examples to make the point. It could use a wider range of Marxist concepts.

Some potentially relevant examples of religious conflict.

A fairly weak ending that really only re-states the question.

Marxist sociologists see religion as an ideological force that justifies and disguises division. Religion has sometimes justified even the most extreme forms of social division. Slavery in the southern states of the USA was explained by a fundamentalist reference to early parts of the Old Testament, as was the system of apartheid in South Africa. Similarly, Hinduism legitimates the caste system of India. This ideological control is vital for the survival of the ruling class, as it is needed to blind people to the reality of their situation. From a Marxist perspective, religion has been an integral part of the way conflict and division is justified in an unequal society, though Marxists argue that the root cause of conflict is class exploitation.

There have been many examples of religion causing social change and conflict. Sectarian violence in Northern Ireland, the 9/11 attacks, Hindu-Muslim violence in parts of India and others all show that religion can be the basis of a lot of violence and division in society.

In conclusion, religion seems to operate in a variety of ways. In some cases it acts as a kind of social glue keeping society together. However, it is clear from the examples given that religion is capable of being the basis for division.　　$\frac{20}{33}$

How to turn this into a top-mark answer

This is a reasonably good answer. Most of the content is relevant to the question, the examples given are appropriate and there are a few instances of explicit evaluation. The sociological content is also generally sound. However, there are several things Brenda could do to boost her marks.

Balance
The answer is a bit unbalanced – there is more on religion acting as a social glue than on religion as a source of division, so this side needs strengthening to gain a better mark.

Feminist theories
One way to boost the 'division' side is to bring some feminist theory and evidence into the answer. You could discuss the role of patriarchal ideology as a source of division and a means of legitimating women's subordination. Use examples from different religions to illustrate this. You can also evaluate by reference to cases where religion does not appear to be patriarchal.

The introduction and conclusion
Both the beginning and the end of the essay are weak. The issue of religion bringing about unity, division or both is not really opened up in the essay. It would be very useful to ask whether the claim is more true of multi-faith societies. Similarly, it could be argued that religion can function in both ways simultaneously – binding members of society together but also being the basis of conflict with other societies.

CHAPTER 2 CRIME AND DEVIANCE

1 Functionalist, strain and subcultural theories

Key Issues
▶ What functions might crime perform for society?
▶ How do blocked opportunities result in deviance?
▶ Why are there different types of delinquent subculture?
▶ What are the strengths and weaknesses of functionalist, strain and subcultural theories?

Durkheim's functionalist theory of crime

Analysis
You can demonstrate the skill of Analysis by showing how basic functionalist concepts such as these relate to the functionalist explanation of crime as inevitable and functional.

Functionalists see society as a stable system based on value consensus – shared norms, values, beliefs and goals. This produces social solidarity, binding individuals together into a harmonious unit. To achieve this, society has two key mechanisms:

▶ **Socialisation** instils the shared culture into its members to ensure that they internalise the same norms and values, and that they feel it right to act in the ways that society requires.

▶ **Social control** mechanisms include rewards (positive sanctions) for conformity, and punishments (negative sanctions) for deviance.

Crime is inevitable and universal

Application
You can apply Durkheim's ideas about anomic suicide to illustrate the concept of anomie. Describe how rapid change in modern society can result in suicide as norms become unclear. (See also Topic 10.)

While crime disrupts social stability, functionalists see it as inevitable and universal. Durkheim sees crime as a normal part of all healthy societies:

▶ In every society, some individuals are inadequately socialised and prone to deviate.

▶ In modern societies, there is a highly specialised division of labour and a diversity of subcultures. Individuals and groups become increasingly different from one another, and the shared rules of behaviour become less clear. Durkheim calls this *anomie* (normlessness).

The functions of crime

For Durkheim, crime fulfils two important positive functions:

1 Boundary maintenance

Application
You can apply Stan Cohen's ideas about how the media create and condemn 'folk devils' (see Topic 7) to illustrate the functionalist view of crime and deviance.

▶ Crime produces a reaction from society, uniting its members against the wrongdoer and reinforcing their commitment to the value consensus.

▶ This is the function of punishment: to reaffirm shared rules and reinforce solidarity. E.g. courtroom rituals publicly stigmatise offenders, reminding everyone of the boundary between right and wrong.

2 Adaptation and change

For Durkheim, all change starts as deviance.

▶ For change to occur, individuals with new ideas must challenge existing norms, and at first this will appear as deviance. If this is suppressed, society will be unable to make necessary adaptive changes and will stagnate.

Functionalists identify further positive functions of deviance:

▶ **Safety valve** Davis argues that prostitution acts to release men's sexual frustrations without threatening the nuclear family.

▶ **Warning light** A.K. Cohen argues that deviance indicates that an institution is malfunctioning; e.g. high truancy rates may indicate problems with the education system.

Criticisms of Durkheim

▶ Durkheim claims society requires a certain amount of deviance to function but offers no way of knowing how much is the right amount.

▶ Durkheim and other functionalists explain crime in terms of its function, e.g. to strengthen solidarity. But just because crime does these things doesn't necessarily mean this is why it exists in the first place.

Merton's strain theory

Merton argues that people engage in deviant behaviour when they cannot achieve socially approved goals by legitimate means. His explanation combines:

▶ **Structural factors:** society's unequal opportunity structure.

▶ **Cultural factors:** the strong emphasis on success goals and weaker emphasis on using legitimate means to achieve them.

The American Dream

For Merton, deviance is the result of a strain between the goals a culture *encourages* individuals to aim for and what the structure of society actually *allows* them to achieve legitimately.

▶ For example, the 'American Dream' emphasises 'money success'. Americans are expected to pursue this goal by legitimate means, e.g. education, hard work.

▶ The ideology claims that American society is meritocratic. But in reality, poverty and discrimination block opportunities for many to achieve by legitimate means.

▶ The resulting strain between the cultural goal (money success) and the lack of legitimate opportunities produces frustration and a pressure to resort to illegitimate means.

▶ The pressure is increased by the fact that American culture puts more emphasis on achieving success at any price than upon doing so by legitimate means. Winning the game is more important than playing by the rules.

Deviant adaptations to strain

Merton seeks to explain different patterns of deviance. He argues that an individual's position in the social structure affects how they adapt to the strain to anomie. He identifies five adaptations:

1. **Conformity** Individuals accept the culturally approved goals and strive to achieve them legitimately.

2. **Innovation** Individuals accept the money success goal but use illegitimate means to achieve it, e.g. theft. This is typical of those who lack legitimate opportunities.

3. **Ritualism** Individuals give up on the goal, but have internalised the legitimate means and follow the rules for their own sake.

4. **Retreatism** Individuals reject both goal and legitimate means, and drop out of society.

5. **Rebellion** Individuals replace existing goals and means with new ones with the aim of bringing about social change.

Evaluation
Functionalism assumes crime performs positive functions for society as a whole, e.g. promoting solidarity, but ignores how it might affect individuals within it – e.g. crime obviously isn't functional for its victims.

Analysis
Merton sees American society as tending towards *anomie* (normlessness) in that the norms are too weak to restrain some people from using deviant means to achieve the materialistic goals that American culture sets them.

Interpretation
Show you understand Merton's typology by interpreting his five adaptations correctly in relation to the groups most likely to use them – 1 the middle class; 2 the working class; 3 the lower middle class; 4 addicts, vagrants etc; 5 political radicals.

Evaluation
Merton's theory has been criticised on several grounds. It takes official crime statistics at face value. It is too deterministic: not all working-class people deviate. It ignores the power of the ruling class to make and enforce the laws.

Interpretation
In questions on subcultural theories, it's a good idea to start with a very brief outline of Merton. Although he isn't a subcultural theorist, his work is the starting point for Cohen and others.

Strengths of Merton's approach

Merton shows how both normal and deviant behaviour can arise from the same mainstream goals. Conformists and innovators both pursue the same goal, but by different means.

He explains the patterns shown in official statistics:

▶ Most crime is property crime, because American society values material wealth so highly.

▶ Working-class crime rates are higher, because they have least opportunity to obtain wealth legitimately.

Subcultural strain theories

Subcultural strain theories both criticise Merton's theory and build on it. They see deviance as the product of delinquent subcultures. These subcultures offer their lower-class members a solution to the problem of how to gain the status they cannot achieve by legitimate means.

A.K. Cohen: status frustration

Cohen agrees that much deviance results from the lower classes' inability to achieve mainstream success goals by legitimate means such as education. However, he criticises Merton's explanation:

1. Merton sees deviance as an *individual* response to strain, ignoring the *group* deviance of delinquent subcultures.

2. Merton focuses on *utilitarian* crime for material gain, e.g. theft. He ignores *non-utilitarian* crimes (e.g. assault, vandalism), which may have no economic motive.

Cohen notes that working-class boys face anomie in the middle-class education system.

▶ They are *culturally deprived* and lack the skills to achieve, leaving them at the bottom of the official status hierarchy.

▶ As a result, they suffer status frustration. They resolve it by rejecting mainstream middle-class values and turn instead to others in the same situation, forming a subculture.

Alternative status hierarchy

Evaluation
Unlike Merton, Cohen offers an explanation of non-utilitarian deviance. But he assumes working-class boys start off sharing middle-class success goals, only to reject them when they fail. He ignores the possibility that they never shared these goals and so weren't reacting to failure.

For Cohen, the subculture offers an *illegitimate opportunity structure* for boys who have failed to achieve legitimately.

▶ The subculture provides an *alternative status hierarchy* where they can win status through delinquent actions.

▶ Its values are spite, malice, hostility and contempt for those outside it. The subculture *inverts* mainstream values. What society praises, it condemns; e.g. society respects property, whereas the boys gain status from vandalising it.

Cloward and Ohlin: three subcultures

Cloward and Ohlin agree with Merton that working-class youths are denied legitimate opportunities to achieve and that their deviance stems from their response to this.

But they note that not everyone adapts to a lack of legitimate opportunities by turning to 'innovation' (utilitarian crime). Some subcultures resort to violence; others turn to drug use.

▶ In their view, the key reason for these differences is not only unequal access to the *legitimate* opportunity structure, but unequal access to *illegitimate* opportunity structures. For example, not everyone who fails at school can become a successful safecracker.

▶ Different neighbourhoods provide different illegitimate opportunities to learn criminal skills and develop criminal careers. They identify three types of subcultures that result.

Analysis

Point out the similarities and differences between criminal and retreatist subcultures and Merton's ideas of innovation and retreatism.

1 Criminal subcultures

These provide youths with an apprenticeship in *utilitarian* crime. They arise in neighbourhoods where there is a longstanding, stable criminal culture and a hierarchy of professional adult crime.

▶ Adult criminals can select and train those youths with the right abilities and provide them with opportunities on the criminal career ladder.

2 Conflict subcultures

These arise in areas of high population turnover that prevent a stable professional criminal network developing. The only illegitimate opportunities are within loosely organised gangs.

▶ *Violence* provides a release for frustration at blocked opportunities and an alternative source of status earned by winning 'turf' from rival gangs.

Interpretation

If a question asks you about delinquent or deviant subcultures, you should identify and discuss the full range of types of subculture described by Cohen and Cloward and Ohlin.

3 Retreatist subcultures

The 'double failures' who fail in both the legitimate and the illegitimate opportunity structures often turn to a retreatist or 'dropout' subculture based on illegal drug use.

Evaluation of Cloward and Ohlin

▶ Like Merton and Cohen, Cloward and Ohlin ignore crimes of the wealthy and the wider power structure, and over-predict the amount of working-class crime.

▶ But, unlike Cohen, they try to explain different *types* of working-class deviance in terms of different subcultures.

Application

South uses the example of the drugs trade. This combines the 'disorganised' crime of gangs (the conflict subculture) with organised 'mafia-style' professional crime (the criminal subculture).

▶ They draw the boundaries too sharply between the different types. Actual subcultures often show characteristics of more than one 'type'.

▶ Like Cohen's theory, Cloward and Ohlin's is a *reactive* one – they explain deviant subcultures as forming in reaction to the failure to achieve mainstream success goals. This wrongly assumes that everyone starts off sharing these same goals.

ONE TO TRY

Read Item A and answer the question that follows.

Item A According to Merton, deviance results from a 'strain' between the culturally approved goals that society sets its members and the legitimate means of achieving them. Merton predicts that deviance will occur if society fails to provide its members with legitimate ways of achieving the goals that it sets for them. Deviance may also result if society lays more emphasis on achieving these goals by any means necessary, rather than 'playing by the rules'.

Question Using material from **Item A** and elsewhere, assess Merton's strain theory of deviance.   (21 marks)

Examiner's Advice Start by giving an account of Merton's theory, building it around his key concepts, such as culturally approved goals, legitimate means, strain, the opportunity structure, the conformist and deviant adaptations to strain (innovation, ritualism, retreatism and rebellion) etc.

You can assess the theory by referring to the way subcultural strain theorists (A.K. Cohen, and Cloward and Ohlin) try to build on it, but avoid lengthy descriptions of their work and focus instead on the aspects of Merton that they build on (e.g. utilitarian vs. non-utilitarian crime; innovation/retreatism and criminal/retreatist subcultures). Also include criticisms such as that Merton takes the official statistics at face value, fails to explain crimes of the powerful etc.

2 Labelling Theory

Key Issues
▶ Why does labelling theory see deviance as a social construct?
▶ How does labelling lead to further deviance?
▶ What are the implications for crime statistics?

The social construction of deviance

For labelling theorists, no act is deviant in itself: deviance is simply a social construct.

▶ According to Becker (1963), social groups create deviance by creating rules and applying them to particular people whom they label as 'outsiders'.

▶ Thus an act or a person only becomes deviant when labelled by others as deviant.

Differential enforcement

▶ Labelling theorists argue that social control agencies (police, courts etc) tend to label certain groups as criminal.

▶ Piliavin and Briar (1964) found police decisions to arrest were based on stereotypical ideas about manner, dress, gender, class, ethnicity, time and place.

Typifications

Cicourel (1976) argues that police use typifications (stereotypes) of the 'typical delinquent'. Individuals fitting the typification are more likely to be stopped, arrested and charged:

▶ **Working-class and ethnic minority juveniles** are more likely to be arrested. Once arrested, those from broken homes etc are more likely to be charged.

▶ **Middle-class juveniles** are less likely to fit the typification, and have parents who can negotiate successfully on their behalf. They are less likely to be charged.

Crime statistics: a topic not a resource

Working-class people fit police typifications, so police patrol working-class areas, resulting in more working-class arrests.

▶ Thus crime statistics recorded by the police do not give a valid picture of crime patterns.

▶ Cicourel argues that we cannot take crime statistics at face value or use them as a *resource* (source of facts). We should treat them as a *topic* and investigate the processes by which they are constructed.

The effects of labelling

Labelling theorists are also interested in the effects of labelling. Lemert (1972) argues that, by labelling certain people as deviant, society actually encourages them to become more so: societal reaction causes 'secondary deviance'.

Primary and secondary deviance

Primary deviance is deviant acts that have not been publicly labelled. They have many causes, are often trivial and mostly go uncaught. Those who commit them do not usually see themselves as deviant.

Interpretation
Labelling theory's interest in interactions between law enforcement agents and suspects derives from the interactionist perspective, which focuses on how meanings are created through micro-level, face-to-face interactions and negotiations.

Evaluation
Marxists criticise labelling theory for failing to locate the origin of such labels in the unequal structure of capitalist society.

Analysis
Use the concepts of topic and resource to explain why labelling theorists see official crime statistics as more a record of the activities of control agents than of criminals.

Evaluation
Labelling theory fails to explain why people commit primary deviance in the first place, before they are labelled.

Secondary deviance results from societal reaction, i.e. from labelling. Labelling someone as an offender can involve stigmatising and excluding them from normal society. Others may see the offender solely in terms of the label, which becomes the individual's *master status* or controlling identity.

Self-fulfilling prophecy (SFP)

▶ Being labelled may provoke a crisis for the individual's *self-concept* and lead to a SFP in which they live up to the label, resulting in *secondary* deviance.

▶ Further societal reaction may reinforce the individual's outsider status and lead to them joining a *deviant subculture* that offers support, role models and a *deviant career*.

Young's (1971) study of hippy marijuana users illustrates these processes.

▶ Drug use was initially peripheral to the hippies' lifestyle (primary deviance), but police persecution of them as junkies (societal reaction) led them to retreat into closed groups, developing a deviant subculture where drug use became a central activity (self-fulfilling prophecy).

▶ The control processes aimed at producing law-abiding behaviour thus produced the opposite.

Deviance amplification spiral

In a deviance amplification spiral, the attempt to control deviance leads to it increasing rather than decreasing – resulting in greater attempts to control it and, in turn, yet more deviance, in an escalating spiral, as with the hippies described by Young.

Folk devils and moral panics Cohen's (1972) study of the mods and rockers uses the concept of deviance amplification spiral:

▶ *Media exaggeration and distortion* began a moral panic, with growing public concern.

▶ *Moral entrepreneurs* called for a 'crackdown'. Police responded by arresting more youths, provoking more concern.

▶ Demonising the mods and rockers as 'folk devils' *marginalised* them further, resulting in more deviance.

The work of Cohen and Young points to a key difference with functionalism:

▶ **Functionalists** see deviance producing social control.

▶ **Labelling theorists** see control producing further deviance.

ONE TO TRY

Read Item A and answer the question that follows.

Item A According to Lemert, deviance is the result of societal reaction. When an act is publicly defined as deviant, the person who committed it may be stigmatised, shamed and shunned by others. As a result of being treated as an 'outsider' in this way, the individual may be driven to seek the company of other similarly excluded individuals, joining a deviant subculture where they can find support, status and opportunities to live up to their label. In short, deviance is the result of a self-fulfilling prophecy.

Question Using material from **Item A** and elsewhere, assess the view that the concept of the self-fulfilling prophecy does not provide us with a satisfactory understanding of the nature of deviance.   (21 marks)

Examiner's Advice Use Item A to analyse the part that the self-fulfilling prophecy (SFP) plays in the process by which secondary deviance is socially constructed. Introduce other concepts, such as primary deviance, labelling, self-concept, master status, deviance amplification and moral entrepreneurs into your account and show how they link to the idea of the SFP. Use relevant studies (e.g. Young, Cohen) to illustrate these concepts. Evaluate by considering criticisms, e.g. that the SFP is deterministic, doesn't account for primary deviance, ignores structural causes etc.

3 Marxist theories

Key Issues

▶ Why and how might capitalism be a cause of crime?

▶ How do traditional Marxist and neo-Marxist views of crime differ?

▶ What are the strengths and weaknesses of Marxist theories of crime?

There are two main Marxist approaches to crime and the law:

▶ Traditional or classical Marxism

▶ Neo-Marxism or Critical Criminology.

Traditional Marxism

Traditional Marxism sees capitalist society as divided into the ruling capitalist class, who own the means of production, and the working class, whose labour capitalists exploit for profit.

Marxism is a structural theory: society is a structure whose capitalist economic base determines the superstructure, i.e. all other social institutions, including the state, the law and the criminal justice system. Their function is to serve ruling-class interests.

For traditional Marxists, the structure of capitalism explains crime.

Criminogenic capitalism

Crime is inevitable in capitalism, because capitalism is *criminogenic* – its very nature causes crime.

Working-class crime Capitalism is based on the exploitation of the working class for profit. As a result:

▶ Poverty may mean crime is the only way some can survive.

▶ Crime may be the only way of obtaining consumer goods encouraged by capitalist advertising, resulting in utilitarian crimes, e.g. theft.

▶ Alienation may cause frustration and aggression, leading to non-utilitarian crimes, e.g. violence, vandalism.

Ruling-class crime Capitalism is a win-at-all-costs system of competition, while the profit motive encourages greed. This encourages capitalists to commit corporate crimes, e.g. tax evasion, breaking health and safety laws.

As Gordon (1976) argues, crime is a rational response to capitalism and thus is found in all classes.

The state and law making

Marxists see law making and enforcement as serving the interests of the capitalist class. Chambliss (1975) argues that laws to protect private property are the basis of the capitalist economy.

The ruling class also have the power to prevent the introduction of laws harmful to their interests. Few laws challenge the unequal distribution of wealth.

Selective enforcement

While all classes commit crime, there is *selective enforcement* of the law.

▶ Reiman (2001) shows that crimes of the powerful are much less likely to be treated as criminal offences and prosecuted. Carson (1971), in a sample of 200 firms, found all had broken health and safety laws, yet only 1.5% of cases were prosecuted.

Evaluation

Marxism is too deterministic and over-predicts working-class crime: not all poor people commit crime, despite poverty and alienation. Furthermore, not all capitalist societies have high crime rates; e.g. Japan has much less crime than America.

Analysis

Marxism shows the link between the law and the interests of capitalism. This puts labelling theory's insights on selective enforcement of the law into a wider structural context.

Interpretation
Although the criminal justice system does sometimes act against the capitalist class, e.g. occasionally prosecuting corporate crime, Marxists interpret this as an ideological function to make the system appear impartial.

Application
Slapper and Tombs (1999) apply the traditional Marxist view to corporate crime, which they argue is under-policed and rarely prosecuted. This encourages companies to use crime as a means of making profit, often at the expense of workers or consumers.

Application
Critical criminology has influenced other sociologists. Hall et al (1978) use a combination of Marxism and labelling theory to explain how the moral panic over mugging in the 1970s served capitalist interests.

Evaluation
Feminists criticise both traditional and Neo-Marxist approaches for being 'gender blind'. Others criticise traditional Marxism for largely ignoring non-property crime and deviance. Left realists criticise Neo-Marxism for romanticising working-class criminals as 'Robin Hoods' fighting capitalism.

▶ By contrast, there is a much higher rate of prosecutions for the crimes of the poor.

Ideological functions of crime and law

Crime and the law perform ideological functions for capitalism.

▶ Some laws benefit workers, e.g. health and safety. However, Pearce (1976) argues that these also benefit capitalism. By giving it a 'caring' face, they create false consciousness.

▶ Because the state enforces the law selectively, crime appears to be largely working-class. This divides the working class, encouraging workers to blame working-class criminals for their problems, rather than capitalism.

▶ Selective enforcement distorts the crime statistics. By making crime appear largely working-class, it shifts attention from more serious ruling-class crime.

Neo-Marxism: critical criminology

Neo-Marxists Taylor, Walton and Young (1973) agree with traditional Marxists that:

▶ Capitalism is based on exploitation and inequality. This is the key to understanding crime.

▶ The state makes and enforces laws in the interests of capitalism and criminalises the working class.

▶ Capitalism should be replaced by a classless society, which would greatly reduce crime.

However, Taylor et al criticise traditional Marxism for its determinism; e.g. it sees workers as driven to commit crime out of economic necessity. They reject this view, along with other theories that claim crime is caused by external factors, e.g. anomie, blocked opportunities.

Voluntarism

Instead, Taylor et al take a more *voluntaristic* view (the idea that we have free will): crime is a conscious choice often with a *political motive*, e.g. to redistribute wealth from the rich to the poor. Criminals are deliberately struggling to change society.

A fully social theory of deviance

Taylor et al aim to create a 'fully social theory of deviance' – a comprehensive theory that would help to change society for the better. This theory would have two main sources:

▶ Traditional Marxist ideas about the unequal distribution of wealth and who has power to make and enforce the law.

▶ Labelling theory's ideas about the meaning of the deviant act for the actor, societal reactions to it, and the effects of the deviant label on the individual.

ONE TO TRY

Read Item A and answer the question that follows.

Item A Traditional Marxists see capitalist society as the basic cause of crime because it is the source of poverty, greed and self-interest. Although from the official crime statistics it appears as if the working class are responsible for most crime, in reality crime is found throughout all social classes. Marxists also see the law as performing important functions for capitalism. Not only does it protect capitalists' property; it also performs ideological functions.

By contrast, Neo-Marxists take a less deterministic view of working-class crime and see it as often having an anti-capitalist political motivation.

Question Using material from **Item A** and elsewhere, assess the view that crime is the product of capitalism. (21 marks)

Examiner's Advice Outline the traditional Marxist view of the link between crime and capitalism, focusing on concepts and issues such as the criminogenic nature of capitalism, ruling-class crime, law-making, selective enforcement and the ideological functions of crime and the law. Evaluate traditional Marxism, e.g. from a Neo-Marxist standpoint. Also consider criticisms of Neo-Marxism, e.g. from left realists.

4 Realist theories

Key Issues

▶ How do realist theories different from other approaches to crime?

▶ What are the similarities and differences between left and right realism?

▶ What are the strengths and limitations of left and right realism?

Realist theories differ from labelling theory and critical criminology, which see crime as socially constructed, rather than a real fact. Realists see crime as a real problem, especially for its victims, and they propose policies to reduce crime.

Realist approaches divide along political lines:

▶ **Right realists** share a conservative, New Right political outlook and support a 'zero tolerance' stance on crime. They have been very influential in the UK and USA.

▶ **Left realists** are reformist socialists and favour policies to promote equality.

Right Realism

Right realism (RR) sees crime, especially street crime, as a growing problem.

Attitude to other theories Right realists (RRs) believe other theories have failed to solve the problem of crime. They regard labelling theory and critical criminology as too sympathetic to the criminal and hostile to the police and courts.

Practical solutions RRs are mainly concerned with practical solutions to reduce crime. In their view, the best way to do so is through control and punishment, rather than by rehabilitating offenders or tackling causes such as poverty.

The causes of crime

▶ RRs reject the idea that structural or economic factors such as poverty are the cause of crime; e.g. they point out that the old tend to be poor yet have a very low crime rate.

▶ For RRs, crime is the product of three factors: *biological differences, inadequate socialisation and the underclass*, and *rational choice to offend*.

1 Biological differences

According to Wilson and Herrnstein (1985), crime is caused by a combination of biological and social factors.

▶ Biological differences between individuals make some people innately predisposed to commit crime, due to personality traits such as aggressiveness, risk-taking or low intelligence, which RRs see as biologically determined.

2 The underclass

Effective socialisation decreases the risk of offending by teaching self-control and correct values. RRs see the nuclear family as the best agency of socialisation.

▶ However, according to Murray (1990), the nuclear family is being undermined by the welfare state, which is creating welfare dependency and encouraging the growth of an underclass who fail to socialise their children properly.

▶ Generous welfare provision has led to the growth of benefit-dependent lone parent families, since men no longer need to take responsibility for supporting their families.

Analysis
In this topic, one way that you can demonstrate the skill of Analysis is by showing you understand the similarities and differences between the two versions of realism: Both see crime as a problem and offer solutions. But their solutions to crime differ, as do their views of its causes.

Evaluation
Critics argue that evidence for intelligence being biologically determined is limited. Even if it is, it may not explain offending; Lilly et al (2002) found that differences in intelligence accounted for only 3% of the difference in offending.

Interpretation
Put right realist ideas into the wider context ·of the New Right perspective on society; e.g. New Right views on the family and social policy help us interpret their views on crime.

▶ Absent fathers mean that boys lack discipline and an appropriate role model, so they turn to delinquent role models in street gangs and gain status through crime rather than through supporting their families.

3 Rational choice theory

Clarke's (1980) rational choice theory assumes individuals are rational beings with free will.

▶ Deciding to commit crime is a *choice* based on a rational calculation of the consequences.

▶ If the rewards of crime appear to outweigh the costs, then people will be more likely to offend. RRs argue that the crime rate is high because the perceived costs are low; e.g. little risk of being caught and lenient punishments.

Felson's (1998) *routine activity theory* argues that for crime to occur, there must be:

▶ A motivated offender, a suitable target (victim or property) and the absence of a 'capable guardian' (e.g. policeman or neighbour).

▶ Offenders act rationally, so the presence of a guardian is likely to deter them.

Solutions to crime

RRs believe it is pointless trying to tackle the underlying causes of crime (biological and socialisation differences) since these are hard to change. Instead, they focus on the control and punishment of offenders:

▶ Wilson and Kelling (1982) argue that we must keep neighbourhoods orderly to prevent crime taking hold. Any sign of deterioration, e.g. graffiti, must be dealt with immediately.

▶ They advocate 'zero tolerance' policing. The police should focus on controlling the streets so law-abiding citizens feel safe.

▶ Crime prevention policies should reduce the rewards of crime and increase its costs, e.g. 'target hardening', more use of prison (see Topic 9).

Criticisms of right realism

▶ It ignores structural causes of crime, e.g. poverty.

▶ It is concerned almost solely with street crime, ignoring corporate crime, which is more costly and harmful to the public.

▶ It over-emphasises control of disorderly neighbourhoods, ignoring underlying causes of neighbourhood decline.

Left realism

Left realism (LR) has developed since the 1980s. Like RR, it sees crime as a real problem. However, while RRs are New Right conservatives, LRs are socialists.

▶ **Like Marxists**, LRs are opposed to the inequality of capitalist society and see it as the root cause of crime.

▶ **Unlike Marxists**, they are reformist not revolutionary socialists: they believe gradual reforms are the only realistic way to achieve equality.

▶ While Marxists believe only a future revolution can bring a crime-free society, LRs believe we need realistic solutions for reducing it now.

Criticisms of other theories

LRs accuse other sociologists of not taking crime seriously:

▶ **Traditional Marxists** concentrate on crimes of the powerful but neglect working-class crime and its effects.

▶ **Neo-Marxists** romanticise working-class criminals (see Topic 3), whereas in reality they mostly victimise other working-class people.

Sidebar (left margin)

Evaluation
How can criminals be both rational actors freely *choosing* crime, while simultaneously their behaviour is *determined* by their biology and socialisation?

Application
Use examples to show your grasp of Wilson and Kelling's 'broken windows' thesis – e.g. removing graffiti; moving vagrants on; cracking down on drunkenness, littering etc.

Evaluation
Zero tolerance policies allow police to discriminate against ethnic minority youth, the homeless etc. They also result in displacement of crime to other areas.

Application
Right realism could be used to explain some professional utilitarian crime, which may often involve rational cost-benefit calculations. By contrast, it is harder to apply it to violent crime that results from an irrational outburst.

▶ **Labelling theorists** see criminals as the victims of labelling. LRs argue that this neglects the real victims.

For LRs, taking crime seriously involves recognising that:

▶ **Its main victims are disadvantaged groups:** the working class, ethnic minorities and women. They are more likely to be victimised and less likely to find the police take crimes against them seriously (e.g. racist attacks, domestic violence).

▶ **There has been a real increase in crime.** This has led to an *aetiological crisis* (crisis of explanation); e.g. labelling theory sees the rise as just a social construction, not a reality. LRs argue that the increase is too great to be explained in this way and is real.

The causes of crime

Lea and Young (1984) identify three related causes of crime:

1 Relative deprivation

For LR, crime has its roots in relative deprivation – how deprived someone feels *in relation to others*. When they feel others unfairly have more, they may resort to crime to obtain what they feel entitled to.

There is a growing contrast between cultural inclusion and economic exclusion and this increases relative deprivation:

▶ There is cultural inclusion: even the poor have access to the media's materialistic messages.

▶ But there is economic exclusion of the poor from opportunities to gain the 'glittering prizes'.

2 Subculture

For LR, a subculture is a group's solution to the problem of relative deprivation.

▶ Some subcultural solutions do not lead to crime; e.g. some turn to religion to find comfort and this may encourage conformity.

▶ Criminal subcultures subscribe to society's materialistic goals, but legitimate opportunities are blocked, so they resort to crime.

3 Marginalisation

Unlike groups such as workers, unemployed youth are marginalised. They have no organisation to represent them and no clear goals – just a sense of powerlessness, resentment and frustration, which they express through criminal means, e.g. violence and rioting.

Late modernity and crime

Young (2002) argues that in late modern society (since the 1970s), the problem of working-class crime is worse, due to:

▶ Harsher welfare policies, increased unemployment, job insecurity and poverty.

▶ Destabilisation of family and community life, weakening informal social controls.

Young notes other changes in late modernity:

▶ Crime is now found throughout society, not just at the bottom. There is resentment at the undeservedly high rewards, e.g. of footballers or bankers.

▶ There is now 'relative deprivation downwards'; e.g. resentment against the unemployed as spongers; more 'hate crimes' e.g. against asylum seekers.

▶ There is less consensus about what is acceptable and unacceptable behaviour, and informal controls are now less effective as families and communities disintegrate.

▶ The public are less tolerant and demand harsher formal controls by the state. Late modern society is a high-crime society with a low tolerance for crime.

Analysis
This is similar to Merton's notion of anomie: society creates crime by setting cultural goals (e.g. material wealth) but denies people the opportunity to achieve them by legitimate means (e.g. decent jobs).

Analysis
You can link the left realist view of criminal subcultures to A.K. Cohen's and Cloward and Ohlin's idea of deviant subcultures as a reaction to the failure to achieve mainstream goals (see Topic 1).

Interpretation
Put Young's views into a theoretical context by explaining that in late modernity, trends typical of modern society, such as individualism, the decline of community etc become more intense.

Solutions to crime

The LR solution to crime involves two policies: democratic policing and reducing social inequality.

Democratic policing

▶ Kinsey, Lea and Young (1986) argue that police rely on the public for information, but they are losing public support, so the flow of information dries up and they must rely instead on *military policing*, such as 'swamping' an area.

▶ To win public support, the police must become more accountable to local communities by involving them in deciding policing policies and priorities.

▶ Crime control must also involve a multi-agency approach (e.g. social services, housing departments, schools), not just the police.

Reducing inequality

▶ For LRs, the main solution to crime is to remove its underlying cause: social inequality.

▶ They call for major structural changes to tackle discrimination, inequality of opportunity and unfairness of rewards, and provide decent jobs and housing for all.

Criticisms of left realism

LR has drawn attention to the reality of street crime and its effects, especially on victims from deprived groups. However, it is criticised on several grounds:

▶ It accepts the authorities' definition of crime as being the street crimes of the poor and ignores the harms done to the poor by the powerful. Marxists argue that it fails to explain corporate crime.

▶ It over-predicts the amount of working-class crime: not everyone who experiences relative deprivation and marginalisation turns to crime.

▶ Understanding offenders' motives requires qualitative data, but LR relies on quantitative data from victim surveys.

▶ Focusing on high-crime inner-city areas makes crime appear a greater problem than it is.

ONE TO TRY

Read Item A and answer the question that follows.

Item A Realists regard crime, and especially street crime, as a real and growing problem, and one that has been largely ignored by other theories. However, left and right realists offer very different solutions to this problem, reflecting political differences between them as well as differences in what they see as the cause of crime. For right realists, crime is a rational choice made by individuals that can only be controlled by tough law-and-order policies. For left realists, crime results from relative deprivation and tackling it involves reducing social inequality.

Question Using material from **Item A** and elsewhere, assess the view that realist approaches offer an adequate solution to the problem of crime.　　　(21 marks)

Examiner's Advice You need to examine both left (LR) and right realist (RR) approaches, including their views of the causes of crime as well as their solutions. For RR, look at biological factors, the underclass and rational choice theory as well as solutions such as zero tolerance. For RR, look at relative deprivation, subculture and marginalisation in late modernity, and democratic policing and structural reforms to promote equality. Evaluate both approaches; e.g. both neglect corporate crime and focus too much on working-class crime; RR neglects structural factors and overstates offenders' rationality; LR relies too much on relative deprivation. Comparing and contrasting them with other theories, e.g. labelling, Marxism and strain theory will also develop your analysis and evaluation.

5 Gender, crime and justice

Key Issues

▶ What are the patterns of gender differences in recorded crime?

▶ Does the criminal justice system treat males and females equally?

▶ How can we explain gender patterns in crime?

Gender patterns in crime

Most crime appears to be committed by males. Four out of five convicted offenders are male. Among offenders, a higher proportion of females are convicted of property offences (except burglary), while a higher proportion of males are convicted of violent or sexual offences. Males are more likely to commit serious crimes.

Such statistics of recorded crime raise three important questions:

1. Do women really commit fewer crimes?

2. How can we explain those women who do offend?

3. Why do males commit crime?

Do women commit less crime?

Some sociologists argue that the official statistics underestimate the amount of female offending. Two arguments have been put forward to support this view.

▶ Female crimes are less likely to be reported; e.g. women's shoplifting is less likely to be reported than men's violence.

▶ Even when women's crimes are reported, they are less likely to be prosecuted.

The chivalry thesis

The idea that women are less likely to be prosecuted for their offences is known as the chivalry thesis:

▶ This argues that the criminal justice system (CJS) is more lenient to women, because its agents – police officers, judges, juries etc – are men, who are socialised to act 'chivalrously' towards women.

▶ Pollak (1950) argues that men have a protective attitude towards women, so they are unwilling to arrest, charge, prosecute or convict them. Their crimes are less likely to end up in the official statistics, giving an invalid picture that under-represents female crime.

Evidence for the chivalry thesis

Self-report studies suggest that female offenders are treated more leniently.

▶ Graham and Bowling (1995) found young males were 2.33 times more likely than females to admit to having committed an offence in the previous year – whereas the official statistics show males as four times more likely to offend.

▶ Compared with men, women are also more likely to be cautioned rather than prosecuted.

▶ Hood's (1992) study of over 3,000 defendants found that women were about one third less likely to be jailed in similar cases.

Interpretation
If the question is about why females *appear* to commit more crime than males, you need to discuss the chivalry thesis.

Application
Pollak is suggesting women are positively rather than negatively labelled by male agents of social control as a result of their socialisation. You can apply concepts from labelling theory to this, e.g. stereotyping, typifications, interaction, negotiation (see Topic 2).

Application
It's not enough just to give an account of Pollak's argument. You also need to apply some of the *evidence* for and against it.

Evidence against the chivalry thesis

Analysis
Draw an appropriate conclusion from the evidence for and against the chivalry thesis. What does it tell us about whether we should see crime statistics on gender as 'real' or as a social construction? You could refer to Cicourel's distinction between statistics as a topic and statistics as a resource (Topic 2).

▶ Farrington and Morris' (1983) study of a magistrates' court found women were not sentenced more leniently for comparable offences. Box's (1981) review of self-report studies concludes that women who commit serious offences are not treated more favourably than men.

▶ Buckle and Farrington's (1984) study of shoplifting witnessed twice as many males shoplifting – despite the fact that the numbers of male and female offenders in the official statistics are roughly equal. This suggests women shoplifters are more likely to be prosecuted than male shoplifters.

Bias against women

Feminists argue that the CJS is not biased in favour of women, as the chivalry thesis claims, but biased *against* them. They argue that the CJS treats women more harshly, especially when they deviate from gender norms of monogamous heterosexuality and motherhood.

▶ Heidensohn (1996) notes the double standards of courts punishing girls, but not boys, for promiscuous sexual activity.

▶ Carlen (1997) found Scottish courts were much more likely to jail women whose children were in care than women whom they saw as good mothers.

▶ Walklate (1998) argues that in rape cases it is the victim who is on trial, since she has to prove her respectability in order to have her evidence accepted.

Interpretation
If the question asks about reasons why females *do* commit less crime than males (rather than just appear to) you should focus on these explanations.

Explaining female crime

Overall, women in general do seem to have a lower rate of offending than men. How then can we explain the behaviour of those women who *do* offend? Sociologists have put forward three explanations: sex role theory, control theory and the liberation thesis.

Functionalist sex role theory

Parsons' (1955) functionalist explanation focuses on gender socialisation and role models in the nuclear family to explain gender differences in crime.

Application
Spell out the link between these 'masculine' characteristics and offending; e.g. aggression may lead to fights and a conviction for assault. What offences might risk-taking result in?

▶ Women perform the expressive role at home, including responsibility for socialisation. This gives girls an adult role model, but boys reject feminine models of behaviour that express tenderness, gentleness and emotion.

▶ Instead, boys distance themselves by engaging in 'compensatory compulsory masculinity' – risk-taking, aggression and anti-social behaviour.

▶ Men take the instrumental role, performed largely outside the home. This also makes socialisation more difficult for boys.

▶ According to A.K. Cohen (1955), the absence of an adult male role model in the home means boys are more likely to turn to all-male street gangs as a source of masculine identity. Here they earn status by acts of delinquency.

Evaluation
Walklate (2003) criticises Parsons for assuming that because women are biologically capable of bearing children, they are best suited to the expressive role. Thus, although Parsons claims to explain gender differences in crime in terms of socialisation, his explanation is based on *biological* assumptions about sex differences.

▶ Similarly, right realists argue that the absence of a male role model in matrifocal lone-parent families leads to boys' delinquency (see Topic 4).

Feminist theories By contrast with functionalism, feminists explain gender differences in offending in terms of *patriarchy*. There are two main feminist approaches: control theory (Heidensohn and Carlen) and the liberation thesis (Adler).

Heidensohn: patriarchal control

Heidensohn (1985) argues that women commit fewer crimes than men because patriarchal society imposes greater control over women, thus reducing their opportunities to offend. Patriarchal control operates at home, in public and at work.

Control at home

▶ Women's domestic role, with its constant housework and childcare, imposes severe restrictions on their time and movement and confines them to the house for long periods, reducing their opportunities to offend.

▶ Men are able to impose this role on women, e.g. by the threat of domestic violence and through their financial power.

▶ Daughters are also subject to patriarchal control, e.g. with restrictions on going out or staying out late. Instead, they develop a 'bedroom culture', socialising at home with friends rather than in public spaces. Girls are also required to do more housework, which also restricts their opportunities to engage in deviant behaviour on the streets.

Control in public

▶ Women are controlled in public places by the fear of male sexual violence. Media reporting of rapes helps to frighten women into staying indoors.

▶ Females are also controlled in public by their fear of being defined as not respectable. Dress, make-up, ways of acting etc, defined as inappropriate can gain a woman a 'reputation'. Women on their own may avoid going into pubs – which are sites of criminal behaviour – for fear of being regarded as sexually 'loose'.

Control at work

▶ Women's subordinate position at work reduces criminal opportunities. The 'glass ceiling' prevents women rising to senior positions where there are more opportunities for white-collar crime.

> **Evaluation**
> Carlen's sample was small and possibly unrepresentative, consisting largely of serious offenders, over half of whom were in custody.

Carlen: class and gender deals

Carlen (1988) studied 39 working-class women who had been convicted of a range of crimes. Twenty were in prison or youth custody. Carlen argues that most convicted serious female criminals are working-class.

Hirschi's control theory

Carlen uses Hirschi's (1969) control theory to explain female crime.

▶ Hirschi argues that humans act rationally and are controlled by being offered a 'deal': rewards in return for conforming to norms.

> **Analysis**
> Heidensohn and Carlen combine feminism and control theory. Heidensohn shows how patriarchal controls prevent women offending. Carlen shows how patriarchal society's failure to deliver the promised 'deals' (i.e. controls) to some women leads them to offend.

▶ People commit crime if they don't believe they will get the rewards, or if the rewards of crime appear greater than the risks.

Carlen argues that working-class women are generally led to conform through the promise of two 'deals':

The class deal Women who work will get a decent standard of living.

The gender deal Women who conform to the conventional domestic gender role will gain the material and emotional rewards of family life.

▶ In terms of the *class deal*, the women in Carlen's study had failed to find a legitimate way of earning a decent living. Most had always been in poverty; many could not get a job and had experienced problems claiming benefits.

> **Evaluation**
> Both control theory and feminism tend to see women's behaviour as determined by external forces such as patriarchal controls or class and gender deals. This ignores the importance of free will and choice in offending.

▶ In terms of the *gender deal*, some had been abused by their fathers or partners. Over half had spent time in care, which broke family bonds.

▶ As they had gained nothing from either deal, they felt they had nothing to lose by using crime to escape from poverty.

Application
Use evidence to illustrate Adler's thesis. E.g. the rate of female offending and female share of offences has risen.

The liberation thesis

Adler's (1975) 'liberation thesis' argues that as women become liberated from patriarchy, their offending will become similar to men's. Women's liberation is leading to a new type of female criminal and a rise in the female crime rate.

▶ Adler argues that patriarchal controls and discrimination have lessened and opportunities have become more equal.

▶ As a result, women have begun to adopt traditional male roles in both legitimate (work) and illegitimate spheres (crime).

▶ Women no longer just commit traditional female crimes (e.g. shoplifting, prostitution). There are more women in senior positions at work and this gives them the opportunity to commit serious white-collar crimes.

Evaluation
Criticisms of Adler include that the female crime rate started rising before the women's liberation movement began and that most female criminals are working-class and unlikely to be influenced by women's liberation.

Why do men commit crime?

Evidence strongly suggests that most offenders are men. What is it about being male that increases the likelihood of offending? Attention has focused on the concept of masculinity to explain this pattern.

Messerschmidt: accomplishing masculinity

Messerschmidt (1993) argues that masculinity is an 'accomplishment' – something that men have to constantly work at constructing and presenting to others. In doing so, some men have more resources than others to draw upon.

▶ **Hegemonic masculinity** is the dominant form of masculinity and the one that most men wish to accomplish. It is defined through paid work, the ability to subordinate women (both at home and work) and heterosexuality.

▶ **Subordinated masculinities** Some men, including many lower-class and ethnic minority men, lack the resources to accomplish hegemonic masculinity and so turn to crime. However, Messerschmidt notes that some middle-class men also use crime to achieve hegemonic masculinity, but that in their case it is white-collar or corporate crime.

Interpretation
If a question asks about *gender* and crime, you must consider *both* female and male offending patterns and the debates about them.

ONE TO TRY

Read Item A and answer the question that follows.

Item A According to the official statistics, men commit considerably more crime than women, and male and female offenders tend to commit different types of crime. Sociologists have put forward a variety of feminist and other explanations for these apparent gender differences in offending behaviour.

However, the official statistics may not be a very valid source of information on gender differences in offending. For example, some sociologists argue that female offenders are less likely to be detected, arrested, charged, prosecuted or convicted than their male counterparts.

Question Using material from **Item A** and elsewhere, assess sociological explanations for differences in the patterns of offending between males and females. (21 marks)

Examiner's Advice First of all you should outline the recorded patterns, i.e. what the official statistics say in terms of who commits most offences, and what types and levels of seriousness are associated with each gender. Then evaluate their validity, e.g. by discussing the chivalry thesis and evidence for and against it. You then need to examine some of the explanations for female and male offending, e.g. sex role theory, feminist control theories, the liberation thesis, and the relationship between masculinity and crime. Study Item A and use it to prompt some of your points.

6 Ethnicity, crime and justice

Key Issues
▶ What are the patterns of ethnicity and criminalisation?
▶ Is there evidence of racism in the criminal justice system?
▶ How do sociologists explain the statistical differences in ethnic crime rates – are they real, or a social construction?

Ethnicity and criminalisation

There are three main sources of statistics on ethnicity and criminalisation:

1. Official statistics
2. Victim surveys
3. Self-report studies.

1 Official statistics

These show ethnic differences in the likelihood of being involved in the criminal justice system (CJS).

▶ For example, blacks are seven times more likely than whites to be stopped and searched, and five times more likely to be in prison.

However, victim surveys and self-report studies throw a more direct light on ethnicity and offending.

2 Victim surveys

These ask individuals to say what crimes they have been victims of.

▶ Sometimes they ask respondents to identify the ethnicity of the person who committed the crime against them. For example, in the case of 'mugging', black people are significantly more likely to be identified as offenders.

3 Self-report studies

These ask individuals to disclose crimes they have committed.

▶ Graham and Bowling (1995) found that blacks and whites had almost identical rates of offending, while Asians had much lower rates.

▶ Other self-report studies show similar patterns, discrediting the stereotype of blacks as being more likely than whites to offend.

Overall, the evidence on ethnicity and offending is inconsistent. Official statistics and victim surveys indicate higher rates of offending by blacks, but self-report studies do not.

Racism and the criminal justice system

There are ethnic differences at each stage of the criminal justice process. How far are they the result of racism within the CJS? We need to look at the main stages of the process that an individual may go through.

Interpretation
Such statistics can be interpreted as either that ethnic minorities are more likely to commit an offence or that they are simply more likely to be suspected of committing an offence.

Evaluation
Victim surveys have limitations. They rely on victims' memory. White victims tend to 'over-identify' blacks as offenders. They exclude the under 16s. They exclude crimes by businesses, so they tell us nothing about the ethnicity of corporate criminals.

Policing

Phillips and Bowling (2007) note that there have been many allegations of oppressive policing of minority communities, including:

▶ Mass stop and search operations, paramilitary tactics, excessive surveillance, armed raids, police violence and deaths in custody, and a failure to respond effectively to racist violence.

▶ They note that minorities are more likely to think they are 'over-policed and under-protected'.

Stop and search

▶ Black people are seven times more likely to be stopped and searched than whites.

▶ Asians are over three times more likely to be stopped and searched than other people under the Terrorism Act 2000.

▶ Only a small proportion of stops result in arrest.

These patterns may be explained by:

▶ **Ethnic differences in offending** The patterns may simply reflect the possibility that some ethnic groups are more likely to offend, and that police are acting on relevant information about a specific offence ('*low discretion stops*').

▶ **Police racism** Alternatively, members of minority ethnic groups may be stopped more because of police racism. In *high discretion stops*, police act without specific information and are more likely to discriminate.

▶ **Demographic factors** Ethnic minorities are over-represented in the groups most likely to be stopped *regardless* of their ethnicity, e.g. the young, unemployed and urban dwellers, so they get stopped more.

Arrests and cautions

The arrest rate for black people is over three times the rate for whites. By contrast, once arrested, blacks and Asians are less likely than white people to receive a caution.

Prosecution and trial

The Crown Prosecution Service (CPS) decides whether a case brought by the police should be prosecuted.

▶ The CPS is more likely to drop cases against minorities than against whites, and Black and Asian defendants are less likely to be found guilty than whites.

▶ When cases do go ahead, minorities are more likely to elect for a Crown Court trial by jury, rather than a magistrates' court, perhaps due to mistrust of magistrates' impartiality. However, Crown Courts can impose heavier sentences if convicted.

Sentencing and prison

Jail sentences are given to a greater proportion of black offenders than white or Asian offenders.

▶ Hood (1992) found that even when the seriousness of the offence and previous convictions are taken into account, black men were 5% more likely to be jailed.

▶ Blacks are five times more likely to be in prison than whites. Blacks and Asians are more likely to be serving longer sentences.

▶ When awaiting trial, ethnic minorities are less likely to be granted bail.

Explaining ethnic differences in offending

Official statistics on the criminal justice process show differences between ethnic groups. There are two explanations for these differences: left realism and Neo-Marxism.

Application
You can apply relevant evidence of police racism. The Macpherson Report (1999) found *institutional racism* in the Metropolitan Police.

Analysis
This may be due to the fact that minorities are more likely to deny the offence. Not admitting the offence means they cannot receive a caution and are more likely to be charged.

Analysis
This suggests that the evidence against minority defendants is often weaker and possibly based on police stereotyping.

Interpretation
The debate between these views is partly about whether crime statistics represent facts or social constructs: do they represent real ethnic differences in the patterns of crime (as left realists argue), or are they just social constructs produced by racist labelling (as Neo-Marxists argue)?

1 Left realism

Left realists Lea and Young (1993) argue that ethnic differences in the statistics reflect real differences in the levels of offending.

▶ They see crime as the product of relative deprivation, subculture and marginalisation.

▶ Racism has led to the marginalisation and economic exclusion of ethnic minorities.

▶ Media emphasis on consumerism also promotes relative deprivation by setting materialistic goals that many members of minority groups cannot reach by legitimate means because of discrimination.

Lea and Young recognise that racist policing often leads to the unjustified criminalisation of some members of minority groups.

▶ However, even if the police do act in racist ways, Lea and Young argue that this is unlikely to account for the ethnic differences in the statistics.

▶ Similarly, police racism cannot explain the much higher conviction rates of blacks than of Asians: they would have to be selectively racist against blacks but not Asians to cause these differences.

Lea and Young thus conclude that:

1. The statistics represent real differences in offending between ethnic groups, and

2. These are caused by differences in levels of relative deprivation and marginalisation.

2 Neo-Marxism: black crime as a construct

Neo-Marxists such as Gilroy (1982) and Hall et al (1979) reject the view that the statistics reflect reality. Rather, they are the outcome of a social construction process that stereotypes minorities as more criminal than whites.

Gilroy: the myth of black criminality

Gilroy argues that the idea of black criminality is a myth created by racist stereotypes of African Caribbeans and Asians.

▶ In reality, these groups are no more criminal than any other ethnic group.

▶ But because the CJS acts on these racist stereotypes, minorities are criminalised and therefore appear in greater numbers in the official crime statistics.

Crime as political resistance Gilroy argues that ethnic minority crime is a form of political resistance against a racist society, and this resistance has its roots in earlier struggles against British imperialism.

▶ Most blacks and Asians in the UK originated in former British colonies, where their anti-colonial struggles taught them how to resist oppression, e.g. through riots and demonstrations.

▶ When they found themselves facing racism in Britain, they adopted the same forms of struggle to defend themselves, but their political struggle was criminalised by the British state.

Gilroy's view is like that of critical criminology (see Topic 3), which argues that much working-class crime is an act of resistance to capitalism.

Hall et al: policing the crisis

Hall et al argue that the 1970s saw a moral panic over black 'muggers' that served the interests of capitalism in dealing with a crisis.

▶ Hall et al argue that the ruling class are normally able to rule society through consent.

Application
Hall et al apply the concept of a media-driven moral panic that was originally developed by labelling theory, but they put it into a Marxist framework that sees the panic as functioning to benefit capitalism.

Evaluation
Hall et al are inconsistent: they claim black street crime was not rising, but also that it *was* rising because of unemployment. They don't show *how* the crisis led to a moral panic, or that the public were actually blaming crime on blacks.

Interpretation
You can interpret Bourgois' findings using Cloward and Ohlin's criminal and retreatist subcultures.

▶ But in times of crisis, this becomes more difficult. In the early 1970s, British capitalism faced a crisis: high inflation, unemployment and widespread strikes.

▶ The 1970s also saw a media-driven moral panic about the supposed growth of a 'new' crime – mugging – apparently committed by black youth. In reality, according to Hall et al, there was no evidence of a significant increase in this crime.

▶ The emergence of the moral panic about mugging as a 'black' crime at the same time as the crisis of capitalism was no coincidence. The myth of the young black mugger served as a *scapegoat* to distract attention from the true cause of society's problems such as unemployment – namely the capitalist crisis.

▶ By presenting black youth as a threat to the fabric of society, the moral panic served to divide the working class on racial grounds and weaken opposition to capitalism, as well as winning popular consent for more authoritarian forms of rule that could be used to suppress opposition.

▶ However, Hall et al do not argue that black crime was only a product of media labelling. The crisis of capitalism was increasingly marginalising black youth through unemployment, and this drove some into petty crime to survive.

Bourgois: El Barrio

Bourgois (2000) studied El Barrio, a black and Hispanic community in New York. He argues that discrimination has excluded these groups from legitimate economic opportunities.

▶ As a result of exclusion, they have created an alternative economy that combines legal activities with criminal ones, especially drug dealing.

▶ In parallel with this, an oppositional 'street culture' (or subculture) has developed. This rejects mainstream values and provides people with an alternative source of self-worth.

▶ However, because this subculture also legitimates drug use, it creates new addicts, who turn to violent crime to support their habit, and it undermines family life and community cohesion.

▶ Thus exclusion from mainstream opportunities leads both to crime to earn a living and to a culture that draws individuals into crime through drug addiction.

ONE TO TRY

Read Item A and answer the question that follows.

Item A According to official statistics, there are striking differences in the experiences of different ethnic groups in the criminal justice system. For example, although black people make up less than three per cent of the total population of England and Wales, they account for nearly 16 per cent of all stops and searches and 11 per cent of the prison population. By contrast, white people are under-represented at these stages of the criminal justice process.

Question Using material from **Item A** and elsewhere, assess the view that ethnic differences in crime rates can best be explained by racism in the criminal justice system. (21 marks)

Examiner's Advice You can start by outlining the evidence regarding the treatment of different ethnic groups in the criminal justice system (CJS), e.g. in relation to stop and search, arrest, prosecution, conviction and imprisonment. Distinguish between black and Asian ethnic minorities where relevant. You then need to organise your answer around the issue of whether these patterns are best explained as evidence of racism in the CJS, or simply of different rates of criminality in different groups. You should briefly refer to different sources of statistics (official, victim surveys and self-report studies) and what they can tell us, before examining the strengths and weaknesses of explanations such as Lea and Young, Gilroy and Hall et al.

7 Crime and the media

Key Issues
▶ How do the media portray crime?
▶ In what ways might the media be a cause of crime and of the fear of crime?
▶ What role do the media play in creating moral panics?
▶ What is the relationship between the new information media, crime and social control?

Sociologists are interested in four aspects of the relationship between the media and crime:

▶ How the media represent crime, both in fiction and non-fiction.

▶ The media as a cause of crime and of the fear of crime.

▶ Moral panics and media amplification of deviance.

▶ Cybercrime.

Media representations of crime

Crime and deviance make up a large proportion of news coverage. Williams and Dickinson (1993) found that British newspapers devote up to 30% of their news space to crime.

However, the news media give a distorted image of crime, criminals and policing. For example, as compared with official statistics:

▶ **The media over-represent violent and sexual crime.**

▶ **The media portray criminals and victims as older and more middle-class** than those usually found in the criminal justice system. Felson (1998) calls this the 'age fallacy'.

▶ **The media exaggerate police success** in clearing up cases.

▶ **The media exaggerate the risk of victimisation**, e.g. to women.

▶ **Crime is reported as a series of separate events** without examining underlying causes.

▶ **The media overplay extraordinary crimes** – Felson calls this the 'dramatic fallacy'.

News values and crime coverage

The social construction of news The distorted picture of crime painted by the news media reflects the fact that news is a social construction. As Cohen and Young (1973) note, news is not discovered but *manufactured*:

▶ News doesn't simply exist 'out there' waiting to be gathered in and written up by the journalist.

▶ Instead, it is the outcome of a social process whereby some potential stories are selected while others are rejected.

New values A key element in the social construction of news is the concept of 'news values' – the criteria that journalists and editors use in order to decide whether a story is newsworthy enough to make it into the newspaper or news bulletin.

If a crime story can be told in terms of some of these news values, it has a better chance of making the news. Key news values influencing the selection of crime stories include:

▶ **Immediacy**

▶ **Dramatisation** – action and excitement.

▶ **Personalisation** – human interest stories about individuals.

Interpretation
Some questions could be quite broad, e.g. asking about the range of ways in which the media and crime may be related, whereas others might focus on just one or two aspects, e.g. media representations of crime, or moral panics.

Application
When using examples of how the media portray crime, avoid lengthy descriptions of particular TV programmes etc, and be sure to make clear the sociological concepts that your examples illustrate; e.g. the dramatic fallacy, over-representation, news values etc.

▶ **Higher-status persons** and 'celebrities'.

▶ **Simplification** – eliminating shades of grey.

▶ **Novelty or unexpectedness** – a new angle.

▶ **Risk** – victim-centred stories about vulnerability and fear.

▶ **Violence** – especially visible and spectacular acts.

Fictional representations of crime

Fictional representations from TV, cinema and novels are also important sources of our knowledge of crime, because so much of their output is crime-related.

▶ Mandel (1984) estimates that from 1945 to 1984, over 10 billion crime thrillers were sold worldwide.

▶ About 25% of prime time TV and 20% of films are crime shows or movies.

Fictional representations follow Surette's (1998) 'law of opposites': they are the opposite of the official statistics – and strikingly similar to news coverage.

▶ Property crime is under-represented, while violence, drugs and sex crimes are over-represented.

▶ Fictional sex crimes are committed by psychopathic strangers, not acquaintances.

▶ Fictional cops usually get their man.

However, there are three recent trends:

▶ 'Reality' shows tend to feature young, non-white 'underclass' offenders.

▶ There is an increasing tendency to show police as corrupt, brutal and less successful.

▶ Victims have become more central, with police portrayed as avengers and audiences invited to identify with their suffering.

The media as a cause of crime

There has long been concern that the media have a negative effect on attitudes, values and behaviour – especially on those thought most easily influenced, such as the young, lower classes, and the uneducated. In recent decades, 'video nasties', rap lyrics and computer games have been criticised for encouraging violence and criminality.

There are several ways in which the media might cause crime and deviance, including:

▶ **Imitation** – by providing deviant role models, resulting in 'copycat' behaviour.

▶ **Arousal**, e.g. through viewing violent imagery.

▶ **Desensitisation** through repeated viewing of violence.

▶ **Transmitting knowledge** of criminal techniques.

▶ **Stimulating desires** for unaffordable goods, e.g. through advertising.

▶ **Glamourising** crime.

However, studies have tended to find that exposure to media violence has at most a small negative effect on audiences.

Fear of crime

The media exaggerate the amount of violent crime and exaggerate the risks of certain groups becoming victims, e.g. young women, old people. Does this cause unrealistic fear of crime?

Research evidence to some extent supports the view that the media cause fear of crime. For example, Schlesinger and Tumber (1992) found tabloid readers and heavy users of TV expressed greater fear of going out at night and of becoming a victim.

Analysis
One reason why the news media give so much coverage to crime is that news focuses on the unusual and extraordinary, and this makes deviance newsworthy almost by definition, since it is abnormal behaviour.

Evaluation
Research on the media as a cause of crime or violence often uses lab experiments. While this allows researchers to control the variables involved, the artificiality of the setting undermines validity. Experiments cannot easily measure long-term effects, either.

Analysis
An alternative reading of this finding is that those who are already afraid of going out at night watch more TV just because they stay in more. That is, fear of crime may cause greater media use, not vice versa!

The media, relative deprivation and crime

How far do media portrayals of 'normal' rather than criminal lifestyles encourage people to commit crime?

Left realists Lea and Young (1996) argue that the media increase relative deprivation among marginalised groups.

▶ In today's society, where even the poorest have media access, the media present everyone with images of a materialistic 'good life' as the goal to which they should strive.

▶ This stimulates the sense of relative deprivation and social exclusion felt by marginalised groups who cannot afford material goods.

Moral panics

The media may cause crime and deviance by creating a moral panic. A moral panic is an exaggerated and irrational over-reaction by society to a perceived problem, where the reaction enlarges the problem out of all proportion to its real seriousness. In a moral panic:

▶ The media identify a group as a *folk devil* or threat to societal values.

▶ The media negatively stereotype the group and exaggerate the problem.

▶ Moral entrepreneurs, editors, politicians etc condemn the behaviour of the group, leading to calls for a 'crackdown'.

▶ In turn, this may create a self-fulfilling prophecy, amplifying the very problem that caused the panic in the first place; e.g. setting up special drug squads led the police to discover more drug-taking.

▶ As the crackdown identifies more deviants, calls for even tougher action create a *deviance amplification spiral* (see Topic 2).

The mods and rockers

Stanley Cohen's (1972) *Folk Devils and Moral Panics* examines how the media's response to disturbances between two groups of teenagers, the mods and the rockers, created a moral panic.

▶ In the early stages, distinctions were not clear cut and not many young people identified themselves as belonging to either 'group'.

▶ The initial confrontations started on Easter weekend 1964 at Clacton, with a few scuffles and minor property damage.

The media over-reaction to these events involved three elements:

▶ **Exaggeration and distortion** The media exaggerated the numbers and seriousness, distorting the picture through sensational headlines.

▶ **Prediction** The media predicted further conflict and violence would result.

▶ **Symbolisation** The symbols of the mods and rockers (clothes, bikes and scooters etc) were negatively labelled.

The deviance amplification spiral

The media's portrayal of events produced a deviance amplification spiral in two ways:

1. By making it appear that the problem was getting out of hand.

   ▶ This led to calls for an increased *control response* from the police and courts.

   ▶ This produced further *stigmatisation* of the mods and rockers as deviants.

2. By defining the two groups and emphasising their supposed differences.

   ▶ This led to more youths adopting these *identities* and drew in more participants for future clashes.

▶ This encouraged polarisation and created a *self-fulfilling prophecy* as youths acted out the roles the media had assigned to them.

▶ Cohen notes that the media's *definition of the situation* is crucial in creating a moral panic, because in large-scale modern societies, most people have no personal experience of the events and must rely on the media for information.

▶ Cohen argues that moral panics are a result of a *boundary crisis*, where there is uncertainty about where the boundary lies between acceptable and unacceptable behaviour in a time of change. The folk devil gives a focus to popular anxieties about disorder.

Perspectives on moral panics

▶ **Functionalism and moral panics** Functionalists see moral panics as ways of responding to the sense of anomie (normlessness) created by change. By dramatising the threat to society in the form of a folk devil, the media raise the collective consciousness and reassert social controls when central values are threatened.

▶ **Neo-Marxism and moral panics** Neo-Marxists have also used the concept of moral panics; e.g. Hall et al (1979) argue that the moral panic over 'mugging' served to distract attention from the crisis of capitalism (see Topic 6).

Global cybercrime

Thomas and Loader (2000) define cybercrime as computer-mediated activities that are either illegal or considered illicit, and are conducted through global electronic networks.

As Jewkes (2003) notes, the internet creates opportunities to commit both conventional crimes, e.g. fraud, and 'new crimes using new tools', e.g. software piracy. Wall (2001) identifies four categories of cybercrime: *cyber-trespass*, e.g. hacking; *cyber-deception* e.g. identity theft; *cyber-pornography*, and *cyber-violence*, e.g. text bullying.

Policing cybercrime is difficult partly because of the sheer scale of the internet and because its globalised nature poses problems of jurisdiction.

Surveillance ICT provides police and state with greater opportunities for surveillance and control, e.g. through CCTV cameras, electronic databases, digital fingerprinting.

ONE TO TRY

Read Item A and answer the question that follows.

Item A There has long been concern that the mass media have a negative effect on viewers, especially those groups thought to be most easily influenced, such as children and young people. At different times, the cinema, horror comics, 'video nasties', rap lyrics, computer games and the internet have all been blamed for corrupting youth and encouraging violence and criminality. One fear is that the audience will imitate what they see.

Question Using material from **Item A** and elsewhere, assess the view that the mass media are a major cause of crime and deviance in today's society.   (21 marks)

Examiner's Advice You need to examine a range of ways in which the media might be responsible for causing crime and deviance. One possible way is outlined in the Item, which you should use to consider whether the media are responsible for 'copy cat' crime. You should evaluate this by assessing the validity of the studies used to investigate it. Consider also other ways in which the media may cause crime, especially the left realist argument about relative deprivation and the media, and the idea of media-inspired moral panics causing deviance amplification. You can also look briefly at how the new media (e.g. the internet) might facilitate both old and new forms of crime.

8 Globalisation, green crime, human rights and state crimes

Key Issues

▶ How are globalisation and crime related?

▶ What can sociologists tell us about green crime?

▶ What is the relationship between state crimes and human rights?

Crime and globalisation

▶ Globalisation refers to the increasing interconnectedness of societies: what happens in one locality is shaped by distant events and vice versa.

▶ Globalisation has many causes, including the spread of new ICT and the influence of global mass media, cheap air travel and the deregulation of financial and other markets.

The global criminal economy

Held et al suggest there has been a *globalisation of crime*: the increasing interconnectedness of crime across national borders, and the spread of *transnational organised crime*.

Castells (1998) argues there is a global criminal economy worth over £1 trillion per annum.

▶ This takes many forms, e.g. trafficking arms and nuclear materials, smuggling illegal immigrants, trafficking in women and children, sex tourism, cybercrime, green crime and terrorism.

▶ The drugs trade is worth an estimated $300-400 billion annually at street prices. Money laundering of the profits from organised crime is estimated at $1.5 trillion annually.

Global risk consciousness

▶ Globalisation creates new insecurities or 'risk consciousness'. Risk is now seen as global rather than tied to particular places; e.g. economic migrants and asylum seekers fleeing persecution have given rise to anxieties in Western countries.

▶ One result is the intensification of social control at the national level, e.g. the UK has tightened its border control regulations.

Globalisation, capitalism and crime

From a Marxist perspective, Taylor (1997) argues that globalisation has led to greater inequality.

▶ Transnational corporations (TNCs) can now switch manufacturing to low-wage countries to gain higher profits, producing job insecurity, unemployment and poverty.

▶ Deregulation means governments have little control over their own economies and state spending on welfare has declined.

This has produced rising crime and new patterns of crime:

▶ Among the poor, greater insecurity encourages people to turn to crime, e.g. in the lucrative drugs trade.

Interpretation
Show that you understand how globalisation creates not just new opportunities for existing forms of crime, but also new ways of committing crime and new offences.

Analysis
Explain how the global drugs trade has both demand and supply sides: demand in the West is met by supply from Third World countries where impoverished peasants find drug cultivation more profitable than traditional crops.

Analysis
Left realists see the materialistic culture promoted by the global media encouraging people to think of themselves as individual consumers, thus undermining social cohesion and encouraging crime.

Evaluation

Although Taylor's theory is useful in linking global trends in the capitalist economy to changes in patterns of crime, it doesn't explain why many poor people *don't* turn to crime.

▶ For the elite, globalisation creates large-scale criminal opportunities, e.g. deregulation of financial markets creates opportunities for insider trading and tax evasion.

▶ New employment patterns create new opportunities for crime, e.g. using subcontracting to recruit 'flexible' workers, often working illegally.

Patterns of criminal organisation

As globalisation creates new criminal opportunities, it is also giving rise to new forms of criminal organisation:

1 'Glocal' organisation

Hobbs and Dunningham found that the way crime is organised is linked to globalisation. It increasingly involves individuals acting as a 'hub' around which a loose-knit network forms, often linking legitimate and illegitimate activities.

Application

Use Winlow's study of bouncers to show how postmodern conditions of globalisation and de-industrialisation have created new criminal opportunities and patterns at a local level.

▶ This is different from the rigid, hierarchical 'Mafia'-style criminal organisations of the past.

▶ Although these new forms of organisation have global links (e.g. through drug smuggling), crime is still rooted in its local context. Hobbs and Dunningham conclude that crime works as a 'glocal' system – locally based, but with global connections.

2 McMafia

Glenny (2008) examined 'McMafia' – organisations that emerged in Russia and Eastern Europe after the fall of communism (1989).

▶ The new Russian government deregulated much of the economy, leading to huge rises in food prices and rents.

▶ However, commodity prices (for oil, gas, metals etc) were kept at their old Soviet prices – way below the world market price. Thus, well-connected citizens with access to large funds could buy these up very cheaply and sell them on the world market.

▶ This created a new elite, referred to as 'oligarchs'.

▶ To protect themselves from increasing disorder, oligarchs turned to the new 'mafias' (often composed of ex-state security/secret servicemen from the old communist regimes). These criminal organisations were vital for the entry of the new Russian capitalist class into the world economy.

Green crime

Green crime refers to crimes and/or harms done to the environment, including to non-human animals.

'Global risk society' and the environment

Interpretation

Explain how green crime links to globalisation by showing how threats to the eco-system have increasingly global effects; e.g. a nuclear accident in one country can spread radioactive material over thousands of miles.

Beck argues that most threats to human well being and the eco-system are now human-made rather than natural disasters.

▶ In late modern society, the massive increase in productivity and technology has created new, 'manufactured risks'.

▶ Many of these involve harm to the environment and have serious consequences for humanity, e.g. climate change.

▶ These risks are increasingly on a global scale, so Beck describes late modern society as 'global risk society'.

Green criminology

When pollution that causes global warming is actually legal, is this a matter for criminologists? There are two opposed answers:

Traditional criminology only studies the patterns and causes of law-breaking.

▶ If the pollution is legal, then traditional criminology is not concerned with it.

Green criminology is more radical. It starts from the notion of *harm* rather than the criminal law.

▶ Legal definitions cannot provide a consistent global standard of environmental harm, since laws differ from state to state.

▶ Many of the worst environmental harms are not illegal, so the subject matter of green criminology is much wider than that of traditional criminology.

▶ Green criminology is a form of *transgressive criminology* – it transgresses (oversteps) the boundaries of traditional criminology to include new issues.

Two views of harm

▶ **Nation-states and TNCs** apply an *anthropocentric* (human-centred) view of environmental harm. Humans have a right to dominate nature, putting economic growth before the environment.

▶ **Green criminology** takes an *ecocentric* view that sees humans and their environment as interdependent, so that environmental harm hurts humans also.

Types of green crime

South (2008) identifies two types of green crime:

1   **Primary green crimes** 'result directly from the destruction and degradation of the earth's resources'. South identifies four main primary crimes: air pollution, deforestation, species decline and water pollution.

2   **Secondary green crimes** involve the flouting of rules aimed at preventing or regulating environmental disasters.

Toxic waste dumping

▶ Legal disposal of toxic industrial waste is expensive, so businesses may dispose of it by using 'eco-mafias' who profit from illegal dumping.

▶ Illegal waste dumping is often globalised: Western businesses ship their waste for processing in Third World countries where costs are lower and safety standards often non-existent.

▶ In some cases, dumping is not even illegal, since less developed countries may lack the necessary legislation outlawing it.

State crimes

Green and Ward (2005) define state crime as 'illegal or deviant activities perpetrated by, or with the complicity of, state agencies'.

▶ This can include genocide, war crimes, torture, imprisonment without trial and assassination.

▶ McLaughlin (2001) identifies four categories of state crime: political; economic; social/cultural and crimes by security and police forces.

The scale of state crime

▶ The state's power enables it to commit extremely large-scale crimes with widespread victimisation; e.g. in Cambodia between 1975 and 1978, the Khmer Rouge government killed up to a fifth of the country's entire population.

▶ The state's power also means it can conceal its crimes or evade punishment more easily.

Evaluation
Traditional criminology is criticised for accepting official definitions of environmental problems and crimes. Green criminology is criticised for making subjective value judgments about which actions ought to be regarded as wrong.

Analysis
This approach is similar to the Marxist idea of 'crimes of the powerful'. TNCs and nation-states use their power to define in their own interests what counts as environmental harm.

Application
Link this to the idea of state crimes. State violence has been used against oppositional groups; e.g. in 1985 the French secret service blew up the Greenpeace ship *Rainbow Warrior* to prevent it protesting against French nuclear tests in the Pacific.

Application
Link the idea of state crimes to the Marxist notion of 'crimes of the powerful' and the ability of those with power both to commit more serious crime and to get away with it.

▶ Because the state defines what is criminal and manages the criminal justice system, it also has the power to avoid defining its own harmful actions as criminal.

▶ The principle of national sovereignty makes it very difficult for external authorities (e.g. the UN) to intervene or apply international conventions against genocide, war crimes etc.

Human rights and state crime

State crime can be examined through the notion of human rights.

▶ Although there is no single agreed list of human rights, most definitions include *natural rights*, e.g. rights to life and liberty, and *civil rights*, e.g. the right to vote.

▶ A right is an entitlement and acts as a protection against the power of the state over an individual.

▶ From a human rights perspective, the state can be seen as a perpetrator of crime and not simply as the authority that defines and punishes crime.

Interpretation
In this view, the definition of crime is inevitably political. If sociologists accept a *legal* definition (that crimes are simply whatever the state says they are), they risk becoming subservient to the state that makes the law.

Crime as the violation of human rights

Critical criminologists Herman and Julia Schwendinger (1970) argue that we should define crime in terms of the violation of basic human rights, rather than the breaking of legal rules. States that deny individuals' human rights must be regarded as criminal.

▶ In their view, states that practise imperialism, racism or sexism, or inflict economic exploitation on their citizens, are committing crimes.

State crime and the culture of denial

Stanley Cohen sees the issue of human rights and state crime as increasingly central to both political debate and criminology because of the growing international human rights movement and the increased focus on victims. Cohen argues that states conceal and legitimate their human rights crimes.

▶ **Dictatorships** simply deny committing human rights abuses.

Application
Illustrate the spiral of denial and the neutralisation process by using examples of where states have denied, justified or minimised their crimes.

▶ **Democratic states** have to legitimate their actions, often following a three-stage 'spiral of state denial': firstly claiming 'It didn't happen'; then even if there is proof it did happen, "it" is 'something else' (not an abuse) and finally even if it is an abuse, 'it's justified', e.g. to protect national security.

▶ **Neutralisation theory** Cohen examines the ways in which states and their officials 'neutralise' (deny or justify) their crimes. These include denial of victim, denial of injury, denial of responsibility, condemning the condemners and appealing to higher loyalties.

ONE TO TRY

Read Item A and answer the question that follows.

Item A Crimes against the environment take many different forms. These include illegal dumping of toxic industrial waste, and illegal logging and destruction of the rainforest. However, many actions that harm the environment are not illegal, at least not in every country. Some sociologists argue that this is irrelevant, since we should study all environmental harms, including ones that are legal.

Question Using material from **Item A** and elsewhere, assess sociological contributions to our understanding of the nature of environmental crime.

(21 marks)

Examiner's Advice Structure your answer around a debate between traditional and green criminology, focusing on the issue of whether we should study only actions that break the law, or all environmental harms. Use concepts such as transgressive criminology, anthropocentric versus ecocentric views of harm, global risk society and the global nature of environmental harms. You can also consider the similarities between green criminology and Marxist ideas about crimes of the powerful. You can also look at different types of green crime, e.g. primary and secondary, and examples from the Item.

9 Control, punishment and victims

Key Issues

▶ What are the main crime prevention and control strategies and how effective are they?

▶ What are the main perspectives on punishment? What are the main trends in sentencing?

▶ Who is likely to be a victim and what can sociologists tell us about victimisation?

Crime prevention and control

There are several approaches to crime prevention. These raise the issue of social control – the capacity of societies to regulate behaviour.

1 Situational crime prevention (SCP)

▶ SCP strategies are a pre-emptive approach that relies on reducing opportunities for crime. They target specific crimes by managing or altering the environment and aim at increasing the risks of committing crime and reducing the rewards.

▶ 'Target hardening' measures include locking doors, security guards, re-shaping the environment to 'design crime out' of an area.

▶ Underlying SCP is rational choice theory: the idea that criminals act rationally, weighing up the risks and rewards of a crime opportunity.

▶ SCP measures may simply displace crime, moving it to different places, times, victims, types of crime etc.

▶ This approach may explain opportunistic petty street crime but not white-collar, corporate and state crime. The assumption that criminals make rational calculations may not be true of violent and drug-related crimes.

2 Environmental crime prevention

Wilson and Kelling argue that 'broken windows' (signs of disorder, e.g. graffiti, begging, littering, vandalism) that are not dealt with send out a signal that no one cares, prompting a spiral of decline.

▶ An absence of both formal social control (police) and informal control (community) means members of the community feel intimidated and powerless.

▶ The solution is to crack down on any disorder through an *environmental improvement strategy* (e.g. abandoned cars promptly towed away) and a *zero tolerance policing strategy*. This will halt neighbourhood decline and prevent serious crime taking root.

3 Social and community crime prevention

Rather than emphasising policing, these strategies emphasise dealing with the social conditions that predispose some individuals to future crime.

▶ Because poverty is a cause of crime, general social policies may have a crime prevention role; e.g. full employment policies are likely to reduce crime as a 'side effect'.

▶ The Perry pre-school project in Michigan gave an experimental group of disadvantaged 3-4 year olds a two-year intellectual enrichment programme. The longitudinal study following their progress into adulthood showed far fewer arrests for violent crime, property crime and drugs compared with peers not in the project.

Analysis
Explain how some of these reduce crime; e.g. CCTV increases the effort a burglar needs to make.

Evaluation
However, sometimes this approach does more than simply displacing crime or deviance; e.g. changing from coal gas to less toxic natural gas reduced total suicides – not just those from gassing.

Evaluation
There is some evidence for this approach; e.g. such policies in New York in the 1990s produced a significant fall in crime. However, some claim that this was more to do with increasing police numbers and falling unemployment.

Interpretation
These are longer-term strategies, attempting to tackle the root causes of offending, rather the short-term removal of opportunities for crime.

Punishment

There are different justifications for punishment and they link to different penal policies.

▶ **Deterrence** Punishment may prevent future crime from fear of further punishment.

▶ **Rehabilitation** Reforming/re-educating offenders so they no longer offend.

▶ **Incapacitation** Removing the offender's capacity to re-offend, e.g. by execution, imprisonment.

▶ **Retribution** The idea that that society is entitled to take revenge for the offender having breached its moral code.

Application
Use some examples of policies that reflect these aims, e.g. how anger management courses might rehabilitate violent offenders.

Durkheim: a functionalist perspective

Durkheim argues that the function of punishment is to uphold social solidarity and reinforce shared values by expressing society's moral outrage at the offence.

Durkheim identifies two types of justice, corresponding to two types of society.

1. **Retributive justice** Traditional society has a strong collective conscience, so punishment is severe and vengeful.

2. **Restitutive justice** In modern society, there is extensive interdependence between individuals. Crime damages this and the function of justice should be to repair the damage (e.g. through compensation).

Application
Link this to key functionalist ideas about shared values, moral unity and collective conscience; e.g. public punishment expresses public outrage at crimes, thus reinforcing moral unity.

Evaluation
Durkheim's view is too simplistic: traditional societies often have restitutive rather than retributive justice, e.g. paying off a blood feud.

Marxism: capitalism and punishment

Punishment is part of the 'repressive state apparatus' that defends ruling-class property against the lower classes.

▶ The form of punishment reflects the economic base of society.

▶ Under capitalism, imprisonment becomes the dominant punishment because, in the capitalist economy, time is money and offenders 'pay' by 'doing time'.

Foucault: the birth of the prison

Foucault's (1977) *Discipline and Punish* contrasts two different forms of punishment, which he sees as examples of sovereign power and disciplinary power.

1. **Sovereign power** In pre-modern society, the monarch exercised physical power over people's bodies and punishment was a visible spectacle, e.g. public execution.

2. **Disciplinary power** becomes dominant from the 19th century and seeks to govern not just the body, but also the mind through *surveillance*. Foucault uses the *panopticon* to illustrate this.

▶ **The panopticon** is a prison design where prisoners' cells are visible to the guards, but the guards are not visible to the prisoners. Not knowing if they are being watched means the prisoners must constantly behave *as if* they are. Surveillance turns into *self-surveillance*: control becomes invisible, 'inside' the prisoner.

▶ Foucault argues that other institutions (e.g. mental asylums, barracks, factories, schools) followed this pattern and disciplinary power has now infiltrated every part of society, bringing its effects to the human 'soul' itself.

Evaluation
Foucault's claim of a shift from corporal punishment to imprisonment is over-simplistic and he exaggerates the extent of control; e.g. even psychiatric patients can resist control.

Trends in punishment

1 The changing role of prisons

Pre-industrial Europe had a wide range of punishments, e.g. banishment, fines, flogging, execution. Prison was used mainly for holding offenders *prior* to punishment.

▶ Only later is imprisonment seen as a form of punishment in itself.

▶ In liberal democracies, imprisonment is often seen as the most severe form of punishment but, as most prisoners re-offend, it may just be a way of making bad people worse.

▶ Since the 1980s there has been a move towards 'populist punitiveness'. Politicians call for tougher sentences, leading to a rising prison population. The UK imprisons a higher proportion of people than almost any other country in Western Europe.

▶ Most prisoners are young, male and poorly educated. Ethnic minorities are over-represented.

▶ Garland (2001) argues that the USA and to some extent the UK are moving into an era of mass incarceration. In the USA, over 3% of the adult population now have some form of judicial restriction on their liberty.

2 Transcarceration

There is a trend towards transcarceration (moving people between different prison-like institutions), e.g. brought up in care, then a young offender's institution, then adult prison.

▶ There has been a blurring of boundaries between criminal justice and welfare agencies e.g. social services, health and housing are increasingly given a crime control role.

3 Alternatives to prison

Recently there has been a growth in the range of community-based controls, e.g. curfews, community service orders, tagging.

▶ Cohen argues that this has simply cast the *net of control* over more people. Rather than diverting young people away from the criminal justice system (CJS), community controls may divert them *into* it.

The victims of crime

▶ One definition of victims is those who have suffered harm (e.g. physical or emotional suffering, economic loss) through acts that violate the laws of the state.

▶ However, Christie argues that 'victim' is a socially constructed category; e.g. the stereotype of the 'ideal victim' held by the media, public and CJS is a weak, blameless individual who is the target of a stranger's attack.

There are two approaches to victimology (the study of victims): positivist and critical.

1 Positivist victimology

Positivist victimology focuses on interpersonal crimes of violence. It seeks patterns in victimisation and aims to identify the characteristics of victims that contribute to their victimisation, e.g.:

▶ **Victim proneness**, i.e. the characteristics that make victims different from and more vulnerable than non-victims, e.g. being less intelligent.

▶ **Victim precipitation** e.g. Wolfgang's (1958) study of 588 homicides found that 26% involved the victim triggering the events leading to murder, e.g. being the first to use violence.

2 Critical victimology

Structural factors, e.g. patriarchy and poverty, place powerless groups such as women and the poor at greater risk of victimisation.

▶ Through the criminal justice process, the state applies the label of victim to some but withholds it from others; e.g. when police fail to press charges against a man for assaulting his wife, she is denied victim status.

▶ Tombs and Whyte (2007) show that employers' violations of the law leading to death or injury to workers are often explained away as the fault of 'accident prone' workers.

Patterns of victimisation

Repeat victimisation A mere 4% of the population are victims of 44% of all crimes. Less powerful groups are more likely to be repeat victims.

Class The poor are more likely to be victims, e.g. crime is highest in areas of high unemployment.

Age The young are more vulnerable to assault, sexual harassment, theft, and abuse at home.

Ethnicity Minority groups are at greater risk than whites of being victims of crime in general and of racially motivated crime.

Gender Males are at greater risk of violent attacks; females are more likely to be victims of domestic and sexual violence, stalking and harassment.

The impact of victimisation

Crime may have a serious physical or emotional impact on its victim, e.g. feelings of helplessness, increased security-consciousness, difficulties in social functioning.

▶ Crime may also create 'indirect' victims, e.g. friends, relatives and witnesses.

▶ Hate crimes against minorities may create 'waves of harm' that radiate out to intimidate whole communities, not just the primary victim.

▶ Secondary victimisation: in addition to the impact of the crime itself, individuals may suffer further victimisation in the CJS, e.g. rape victims.

▶ Crime may create fear of becoming a victim even if such fears are irrational; e.g. women are more afraid of going out for fear of attack, yet young men are more likely to be victims of violence.

Analysis
Explain why minority ethnic groups and younger people are at greater risk but more likely to report feeling under-protected and over-policed.

Evaluation
Feminists attack the emphasis on 'fear of crime' for focusing on women's passivity when we should focus on their *safety* – the structural threat of patriarchal violence that they face.

ONE TO TRY

Read Item A and answer the question that follows.

Item A Different justifications for punishment have been put forward and these can be linked to different policies. For example, the idea that punishment is justified as a means of deterring offenders from committing crimes may lead to relatively harsh punishments.

Sociologists argue that there is a relationship between the patterns of punishment and the type of society. For example, Durkheim argues that traditional societies favour retributive justice, whereas modern society favours restitutive justice.

Question Using material from **Item A** and elsewhere, assess sociological explanations of the patterns of punishment found in society.   (21 marks)

Examiner's Advice A useful starting point would be to outline the different justifications for and types of punishment, e.g. deterrence, rehabilitation or reform, retribution, incapacitation, restitution. You should examine a range of different views of punishment and how each relates to wider society. Include Durkheim's ideas (see Item A), as well as Marxist and Foucault's views on the type of punishment to be found in capitalism/modern society. You could also look at some recent trends, e.g. the rising prison population, transcarceration, politicisation of penal policy, alternatives to prison.

10 Suicide

Key Issues

▶ What can sociology tell us about the causes of and reasons for suicide?

▶ What are the main sociological perspectives on suicide?

▶ What are the strengths and weaknesses of different explanations of suicide?

Interpretation
Suicide has been used to demonstrate the value of both positivist and interpretivist perspectives. In questions on this topic, explain the links between the studies and their perspectives.

Durkheim, positivism and suicide

Positivists believe society can be studied scientifically. Science develops laws to explain observed patterns. Durkheim (1897) argued that there are patterns in suicide and their social causes could be discovered. This would prove sociology was a science.

Suicide rates as social facts

In Durkheim's view, behaviour is caused by *social facts* – forces found in the structure of society. Social facts are external to individuals; they constrain individuals, shaping their behaviour, and are greater than individuals – they exist on a different 'level'. For Durkheim, the suicide rate is a social fact.

Using official statistics for various European countries, Durkheim found that:

▶ Different societies have different rates.

▶ Within a society, rates varied between social groups; e.g. Catholics had lower rates than Protestants.

For Durkheim, such patterns show that suicide rates are the result of two social facts:

Evaluation
Durkheim was the first to use multivariate analysis, enabling him to correlate suicide rates with other social factors, e.g. religion, marital status. Without this, it would not be possible to establish cause-and-effect relationships.

▶ **Social integration**: how far individuals experience a sense of belonging to a group.

▶ **Moral regulation**: how far individuals' actions are kept in check by norms.

Durkheim's typology of suicide

This gives four types of suicide:

1 **Egoistic suicide** (too little integration); e.g. Catholics have a lower rate than Protestants because they are more tightly integrated by shared ritual.

2 **Altruistic suicide** (too much integration), where it is the individual's duty to die for the good of the group; e.g. Japanese kamikaze pilots.

Interpretation
In questions on suicide, keep descriptions and examples of typologies fairly brief. Instead, focus on explaining and applying the key concepts of the study or perspective.

3 **Anomic suicide** (too little regulation), where society's norms become unclear or outdated by rapid change, e.g. economic booms and slumps.

4 **Fatalistic suicide** (too much regulation), where society controls individuals completely, e.g. slaves and prisoners.

Different types of society have different types of suicide:

▶ **In modern societies**, individualism is more important, causing *egoistic suicides,* while rapid change produces *anomic suicides*.

Evaluation
Later positivists criticised Durkheim for not operationalising his concepts satisfactorily. Others criticise the unreliability of his statistics: in the 19th century, autopsies were rarely performed, and many states did not collect statistics systematically.

▶ **In traditional societies**, the group is more important, causing *altruistic suicides*. Individuals have rigidly ascribed statuses, causing *fatalistic suicides*.

Interpretivism and suicide

Rather than focus on the *causes* of suicide as positivists do, interpretivists focus on its *meanings* for those involved – the deceased, coroners, relatives etc.

Application
You can apply Douglas' idea to explain the patterns Durkheim found; e.g. socially integrated people only *seem* to have a lower suicide rate because they have relatives etc to persuade the coroner to bring in a different verdict.

Evaluation
Douglas produces a classification of suicide based on the actors' supposed meanings. But why should we believe Douglas is any better than coroners at interpreting a dead person's meanings?

Analysis
Thus when positivists study suicide statistics that show isolated individuals commit suicide, all they will discover is the taken-for-granted assumptions made by coroners; not – as they imagine – social facts about the causes of suicide.

Interpretation
Use these types to interpret examples of suicides sociologically, e.g. the terminally ill patient who is sure that life is over (submissive); playing Russian roulette (thanatation); a lover's rejection has made life intolerable (sacrifice); taking an overdose hoping the lover finds and saves them (appeal).

Douglas: interactionism and suicide

Douglas (1967) takes an interactionist approach. He is interested in the meaning of suicide for the deceased, and the way coroners label deaths.

Suicide statistics Douglas rejects Durkheim's use of statistics.

▶ They are not social facts, as Durkheim believes, but social constructs, based on coroners' interpretations of deaths and influenced by other actors, e.g. family members.

Actors' meanings and qualitative data Durkheim ignores the meanings of the act.

▶ We must classify suicides according to their meaning for the deceased.

▶ To do so, Douglas uses qualitative data: suicide notes, diaries, interviews with survivors and relatives. He believes this will give us a better idea of the real rate of suicide than official statistics.

Atkinson: ethnomethodology and suicide

Atkinson (1978) argues that social reality is simply a construct of its members.

▶ He agrees with Douglas that statistics are merely the result of coroners' interpretations.

▶ But he disagrees that we can find the deceased's meanings and discover the real rate, since neither researchers nor coroners can classify deaths objectively. All we can study is how coroners come to classify a death as suicide.

▶ Atkinson uses qualitative methods: court documents, conversations with coroners, observations of inquests.

He concludes that coroners have a *commonsense theory* about the typical suicide. They take the following as clues indicating suicidal intent and use them to reach a verdict of suicide: *a suicide note* or suicide threats; *mode of death*, e.g. hanging is seen as 'typically suicidal'; *location and circumstances*, e.g. shooting in a deserted lay-by; *life history* e.g. mental illness.

Taylor: realism and suicide

▶ Taylor (1990) agrees with interpretivists that coroners' theories influence their verdicts, so statistics are not valid.

▶ But he accepts the positivist view that we can discover the underlying causes of suicide. He uses case studies to discover the meanings that cause suicide.

Taylor identifies four types of suicide, based on the individual's certainty or uncertainty about themselves or others:

▶ **Submissive suicide** involves certainty about oneself.

▶ **Sacrifice suicide** involves certainty about others.

▶ **Thanatation suicide** involves uncertainty about oneself.

▶ **Appeal suicide** involves uncertainty about others.

ONE TO TRY

Read Item A and answer the question that follows.

Item A For positivists, suicide has social causes. This is why different groups have different rates of suicide. For example, Durkheim found that Protestants have higher rates than Catholics. In his view, this was the result of differences in levels of social integration and moral regulation.

Question Using material from **Item A** and elsewhere, assess the view that we can discover the social causes of suicide. (21 marks)

Examiner's Advice Cover a range of theories, but avoid lengthy descriptions of suicide typologies and focus on the perspectives. Use the Item to build an account of positivism, including social facts, integration, regulation, causal laws and science. Contrast this with the interpretivist emphasis on meanings, making clear the difference between Douglas and Atkinson. Use Taylor to argue that we can find causes, but not by using official statistics.

Practice question and student answer

Read Item A and answer the question that follows.

Item A

Left and right realists share the same starting point: both see crime as a real and growing problem. They both reject the view that rising crime rates are simply due to the way that police record reported crime or enforce the law, for example in a discriminatory way. Furthermore, both approaches focus on street crime and both show concern for the victims of crime, which they argue is lacking from other approaches.

Despite these similarities, however, left and right realism are very far apart in most other respects, in terms of both their diagnosis of the causes of crime and the policy solutions they propose for tackling crime. While one approach blames society, the other blames the individual. Similarly, some argue that one approach wishes to be tough on crime and the other, tough on the causes of crime.

Question

Using material from **Item A** and elsewhere, assess the view that left realism offers a more useful approach to crime and crime control than right realism.   (21 marks)

Student answer by Charlie

> A good start. Charlie uses the Item and builds on it by explaining some of the criticisms of other approaches – though he could note that they differ in what they think is wrong with them.

As Item A points out, left and right realists share a lot of common ground. They both see crime as an important social problem, especially street crime. Also, they both want to solve this problem and they agree that other approaches have failed to either explain crime or come up with realistic solutions. For example, left realists criticise labelling theory and critical criminology for believing that the rising crime rate is just due to police labelling, whereas they argue that the increase is too big to be explained like this. Right realists also criticise these approaches for being too 'soft' on criminals and too critical of the police.

> Charlie correctly identifies and outlines the right realist view of the causes of crime. However, he doesn't fully apply his knowledge: he ought to link inadequate socialisation to lone parent families, the underclass and welfare dependency.

When it comes to what they think the causes of crime are, left and right realists take different views. Right realists think it is more of an individual problem, as Item A says. They believe that it is due partly to genetics – some people are just more inclined to commit crime than others, e.g. some are just born more aggressive. But also it's down to socialisation, which teaches people the difference between right and wrong so they learn to conform. This explains why crime is on the increase, because people aren't being socialised adequately.

> Charlie makes a useful link between rational choice theory and SCP, but doesn't really explain the latter. He could also consider other control strategies favoured by right realists, such as zero tolerance policing and environmental crime prevention.

Right realists also see criminals as rational beings who make decisions about committing crime based on risks and rewards (rational choice theory). If the rewards outweigh the risks, a crime is more likely. This is why right realists support measures like situational crime prevention (SCP) and target hardening.

> Some relevant analysis here in pointing out left realists' debt to Merton, but Charlie needs to explain the key left realist concepts he introduces and link them together.

Left realists take a different approach to crime. Lea and Young see it as caused by factors such as relative deprivation, subculture and marginalisation. This borrows Merton's functionalist idea of blocked opportunities leading to crime. When society tells people to aspire to its goals but they cannot achieve them legitimately, they turn to crime instead.

> This is very relevant knowledge but far too brief and needs developing fully.

According to Young, crime becomes worse in late modern society because of factors such as insecurity, unemployment and individualism. Many people are made poorer, e.g. by de-industrialisation, and they become more individualistic as families break down, leading to more crime.

> Charlie shows a good knowledge of the left realist view of policing here.

When it comes to the solutions to rising crime, left realists take a different line from right realists. Instead of policies like SCP and target hardening, left realists favour more democratic policing. They argue that policing has become militaristic, especially in the inner cities where the crime problem is worst. This means that the public become hostile and distrustful, so they stop supplying the police with information, leading to even more militaristic policing. So the solution is for the public to have more say in the police's priorities, e.g. less policing of minor drugs crime and more policing of racist attacks.

> Good analysis shown in the comparison and contrast with Marxism, but Charlie needs to say more about some of the policies that left realists propose.

However, left realists do not believe this is enough to solve the problem of crime, which they see as having deeper roots. Therefore they favour policies to reduce inequality, since they agree with Marxists that this is the underlying cause of crime, although they believe it is unrealistic to say that we have to wait for a revolution to solve the problem, as Marxists do.

> This is good because it begins to do what the question asks – assess the two approaches against one another. It's a pity, though, that Charlie left this until the end. Also, not having explained the key idea of relative deprivation earlier weakens his point here.

Overall, therefore, although left and right realists are basically concerned with the same problem of crime, their explanation of its causes and their solutions are very different, even opposed. As Item A says, one blames the individual and the other blames society. I think that the right realists are incorrect in blaming individual biological differences and that crime has more to do with inequality and relative deprivation, as Lea and Young argue.

$\frac{15}{21}$

How to turn this into a top-mark answer

Overall, Charlie has produced quite a good answer here. In general, he shows a reasonably good knowledge of the two approaches (although there are some gaps) both in terms of their view of the causes of crime and in terms of their proposed solutions. Charlie makes some useful analytical points in pointing out the debt that left realism owes to Merton, and the similarities and differences between Marxism and left realism. He also makes some relevant use of material from the Item. However, his answer could be strengthened in a number of ways.

Key concepts

Charlie identifies a number of key concepts, including relative deprivation, subculture and marginalisation, but he doesn't explain or apply them fully. Given that these are at the heart of the left realist explanation of crime, he needs to develop them. Other concepts, such as cultural inclusion and economic exclusion, the underclass and welfare dependency, 'broken windows' etc could also be brought into the answer.

Explicit evaluation

More than anything else, explicit (i.e. spelt out) evaluation is what would help this answer to gain full marks. Charlie has spent most of his time giving an account of the views of the two approaches, but he needs to get them debating and arguing with one another to bring out their strengths and weaknesses. You should also discuss specific criticisms of either or both approaches, for example that they are fixated on street crime and neglect white-collar and corporate crime, or that the evidence for biological causes of crime (as argued by right realists) is weak.

Studies

Charlie only refers to two studies. While you don't have to remember the name of every right or left realist, you should be able to show knowledge of a reasonable range of sources. These could include some of the following: Wilson and Kelling; Wilson; Murray; Wilson and Herrnstein; Felson; Clarke, and Kinsey, Lea and Young.

CHAPTER 3 RESEARCH METHODS

1 Experiments

Key Issues
▶ What are the similarities and differences between different types of experiments?
▶ What are their practical, ethical and theoretical strengths and weaknesses?
▶ How useful are experiments in relation to wider issues of methodological preference, science, values and objectivity?

There are three types of experiment to consider:
▶ Laboratory experiments
▶ Field experiments
▶ The comparative method or 'thought experiment'.

Laboratory experiments

The laboratory is an artificial environment where the researcher controls variables to discover their effect, with the aim of discovering a causal law.

▶ The researcher divides a set of identical research subjects into two groups:
▶ **The experimental group** are exposed to a variable (*independent variable*) to test its effect.
▶ **The control group** are not exposed to the independent variable.

However, lab experiments have many practical, ethical and theoretical limitations.

Practical issues

Closed systems Keat and Urry (1982) argue that lab experiments are only suitable for studying *closed systems* where all relevant variables can be controlled.

Individuals are unique We cannot 'match' members of the control and experimental groups exactly.

Studying the past We cannot control variables that were acting in the past.

Small samples Lab experiments can usually only study small samples.

The Hawthorne effect Subjects' behaviour may change because they know they are being studied.

Ethical issues

Informed consent means gaining subjects' agreement to take part, having first explained the nature, purpose and risks of the experiment.

Harm to subjects Research should not harm the subjects without a compelling justification.

Treating subjects fairly Where the experimental group are seen to be benefiting, e.g. pupils gaining from a trial teaching method, this is unfair to the control group.

Analysis
The strength of lab experiments is that direct comparison of the two groups allows us to test hypotheses and discover the cause of differences in behaviour.

Application
Apply the idea of closed and open systems: society is an *open system* where countless factors are at work, making it impossible for the researcher to identify, let alone control, all the relevant variables.

Evaluation
The problem with informing subjects is that often, for an experiment to work, they must be deceived so that they act normally.

Theoretical issues

Positivists favour lab experiments for their reliability. However, even positivists recognise problems. Interpretivists criticise laboratory experiments as lacking validity.

Reliability and hypothesis testing

Reliability is important because replication enables us to check a researcher's results. Positivists regard the lab experiment as highly reliable because:

▶ The original researcher can specify the steps in the experiment, so others can re-run it.

▶ It produces quantitative data, so results can be compared.

▶ It is detached and objective – the researcher just manipulates the variables and records the results.

Representativeness

Representativeness is important to positivists because they aim to make generalisations about behaviour. However, findings may lack representativeness or *external validity*.

▶ Small samples may mean findings cannot be generalised.

▶ Lack of external validity: the more control, the more unlike the real world the experiment becomes.

Internal validity may also be lacking because of the artificiality of the lab environment.

Interpretivism and free will

Interpretivists claim humans are different from natural phenomena. We have free will and choice.

▶ Our actions are based on meanings, not 'caused' by external forces. This means they cannot be explained through the cause-and-effect relationships experiments seek.

Field experiments

Sociologists sometimes use field experiments to overcome the lack of validity of lab experiments.

▶ They differ from lab experiments in two ways: they take place in the subjects' natural surroundings, and the subjects do not know they are in an experiment.

▶ The researcher manipulates variables to see what effect they have; e.g. Rosenthal and Jacobson (1968) manipulated teachers' expectations by misleading them about pupils' abilities.

Actor tests and correspondence tests are field experiments. To test for discrimination in employment, Brown and Gay (1985) sent a white and a black actor for interviews for the same posts. The actors were matched for age, qualifications, etc. so any differences in job offers could have been due to discrimination.

The comparative method

The comparative method is another alternative to lab experiments. It is carried out only in the mind of the sociologist – a 'thought experiment'. It identifies two groups that are alike in all major respects except for the one variable we are interested in. It then compares them to see if this one difference has any effect, e.g. Durkheim's (1897) study of suicide.

Application
Apply the concept of reliability to lab experiments by explaining whey they are replicable.

Analysis
External validity is the problem of whether the experiment's findings hold true for the wider population. If not, they cannot be generalised. Internal validity is the problem of whether the findings are even true of the experimental subjects themselves, e.g. because of the Hawthorne effect.

Interpretation
Field experiments are more natural and valid, but they reduce control over variables.

Evaluation
Field experiments may be unethical because they are carried out without the subjects' knowledge or consent.

Evaluation
Comparative studies avoid artificiality, can study past events and avoid ethical problems, but give the researcher no control over variables.

ONE TO TRY

Question Assess the strengths and weaknesses of using different types of experiments in sociological research. (33 marks)

Examiner's Advice First discuss lab experiments, focusing on issues such as control, artificiality and the goal of discovering cause-and-effect relationships and laws. You should compare and contrast lab experiments with field experiments and the comparative method (e.g. how these two methods overcome the problem of artificiality but with a loss of control). Evaluate the usefulness of each type in terms of practical, ethical and theoretical issues, including reliability, representativeness and validity, and positivist and interpretivist views.

2 Questionnaires

Key Issues

▶ What are the practical, ethical and theoretical strengths and limitations of questionnaires?

▶ What are the main sampling techniques used in surveys?

▶ What is the usefulness of questionnaires in relation to issues of methodological perspective, science, values and objectivity?

Interpretation
Show you know the range of ways questionnaires can be delivered – by post, e-mailed or collected on the spot – and the specific problems each delivery mode has.

Written or self-completed questionnaires are the most widely-used form of social survey, e.g. the Census.

Questionnaires ask respondents to provide answers to pre-set questions. These are usually closed-ended with a limited range of pre-set answers, but sometimes are open-ended, where respondents are free to answer in their own words.

Practical issues

▶ They are a quick, cheap way to gather large amounts of quantitative data from large numbers of people, widely spread geographically.

▶ There is no need to recruit interviewers – respondents complete the questionnaires themselves.

Application
Explain how practical problems link to theoretical or ethical problems; e.g. low response rate affects representativeness as well as cost.

▶ Data is easily quantified and can be computer-processed to reveal relationships between variables.

▶ Data is often limited and superficial because questionnaires need to be fairly brief to encourage people to complete them.

▶ Incentives may be needed to persuade respondents to complete the questionnaire.

▶ With a *postal* questionnaire, you do not know if it was received or who completed it.

▶ Low response rates are a major problem, sometimes caused by faulty questionnaire design, e.g. complex language. A higher response rate can be obtained by sending follow-up questionnaires.

▶ Questionnaires are inflexible and cannot explore any new areas of interest. Questionnaires are only snapshots.

Theoretical issues: positivism

Positivists favour questionnaires. They see them as a representative, reliable, objective and detached method for producing quantitative data, testing hypotheses and developing causal laws.

▶ **Hypothesis testing** Positivists follow the natural science model to discover causal laws. Questionnaires are attractive to positivists because they yield quantitative data about variables. This enables researchers to test hypotheses and to identify correlations and cause-and-effect relationships between variables.

Analysis
Because an identical questionnaire to the original can be used, the questionnaire is a *standardised measuring instrument*. Thus, any differences in the answers are the result of real differences between respondents, not the result of different questions.

▶ **Reliability** (replicability) Other researchers can easily replicate the original research by using the same questionnaire.

Representativeness

▶ Positivists favour questionnaires because they are large-scale, distributed quickly and cheaply by post or e-mail over wide geographical areas and usually use sampling techniques that give a representative sample.

▶ However, representativeness can be undermined by low response rate, especially if those who do return their questionnaires differ in some way from those who don't.

Sampling

Positivists aim to produce generalisations that apply to all cases. But as they cannot study every case, they must choose a *sample* from the population they are interested in.

▶ The sample is drawn from a *sampling frame* – a list of members of the research population.

▶ Different techniques for selecting a sample include: random sampling, where the sample is selected purely by chance; quasi-random sampling, e.g. selecting every 10th name in a list; stratified random sampling subdivides the population into the relevant categories and randomly selects a sample of each. Quota sampling is similar. Researchers look for the right number (quota) of people required in each category.

▶ **Non-representative sampling** (e.g. snowball or opportunity sampling) may be used where there is no sampling frame for the population.

Detachment and objectivity

For positivists, scientific research is objective (unbiased) and detached: values are kept separate from the research and not allowed to 'contaminate' findings. Positivists see questionnaires as a detached, scientific approach, since the sociologist's personal involvement with respondents is kept to a minimum. Unlike in an interview, no researcher is present to influence the answers.

Ethical issues

Questionnaires pose few ethical problems. Even where questions are about sensitive issues, respondents are not obliged to answer them.

▶ Parental consent may be required for questionnaires with children.

▶ Confidentiality is assured, since most questionnaires are completed anonymously.

Interpretivism and questionnaires

Interpretivists seek to discover the meanings underlying our actions and from which we construct social reality. They tend to reject questionnaires because they cannot yield valid data about actors' meanings.

Detachment Interpretivists reject detachment and objectivity because they believe they fail to produce valid data. Instead we need a subjective understanding of actors' meanings.

Imposing the researcher's meanings Interpretivists aim to reveal actors' meanings. Questionnaires prevent this by imposing the researcher's framework of ideas on the respondent (the researcher has already decided what questions are important).

Lying, forgetting and trying to impress create validity problems and the researcher is often unaware how far these issues affect responses.

Question Assess the practical, ethical and theoretical strengths and limitations of using questionnaires in sociological research. (33 marks)

Examiner's Advice Use practical, theoretical and ethical issues as a framework, considering each in turn. Gain analysis marks by showing how they are inter-related. Use the key concepts of validity, objectivity, reliability and representativeness when you examine theoretical issues, as well as putting this into the context of positivist versus interpretivist views. There are few ethical issues, but make sure you mention them. Also refer to different ways of delivering questionnaires (e.g. by hand, post, e-mail) and their strengths and limitations.

ONE TO TRY

3 Interviews

Key Issues

▶ In what ways do structured and unstructured interviews differ?

▶ What are the practical, ethical and theoretical strengths and limitations of different types of interview?

▶ What is the usefulness of interviews in relation to wider issues of methodological perspective, science, values and objectivity?

Types of interview

Interpretation
If a question asks about interviews in general, make sure you discuss the full range of interviews. Link each type to positivism or interpretivism. Point out also that feminists usually prefer to use UIs.

▶ **Structured** interviews (SIs) are like standardised questionnaires. Each interview uses precisely the same questions, wording, tone of voice etc.

▶ **Unstructured** interviews (UIs) are open-ended. The interviewer is free to vary the questions, wording etc.

▶ **Semi-structured** interviews have the same set of questions in common, but the interviewer can also probe with additional questions.

▶ **Group** interviews are relatively unstructured. The researcher asks the group to discuss topics and records their views.

Structured interviews

In SIs, interviewees are asked a fixed set of questions, usually closed-ended with pre-coded answers producing mainly quantitative data. Questions are read out and answers filled in by a trained interviewer. This involves a *social interaction* between interviewer and interviewee.

Practical issues

▶ Structured interviews are quick and cheap to administer to quite large numbers of people.

▶ They are suitable for gathering factual information, e.g. age, job, religion.

▶ Closed-ended questions with pre-coded answers are easily quantified.

Analysis
It is cheaper to train interviewers for SIs than UIs because all they are really required to do is follow a set of instructions.

▶ Training interviewers is relatively straightforward and cheap.

▶ Response rates are usually higher than for questionnaires: people find it harder to turn down a face-to-face request.

▶ Structured interviews are inflexible: the interviewer must stick to the interview schedule, so no new leads can be followed up.

▶ Structured interviews are only snapshots taken at one moment in time.

Ethical issues

There are relatively few ethical problems in using SIs, since questions are generally about less sensitive topics. However:

Evaluation
It can sometimes be difficult to keep interviewees' identity secret as even minimal published details may make them identifiable.

▶ Some interviewees may feel under pressure to answer. Some feminists also regard SIs as potentially oppressive to women interviewees.

▶ Researchers should gain interviewees' informed consent, guarantee confidentiality and make it clear they have a right not to answer.

Theoretical issues: positivism

Hypothesis testing

▶ Positivists model their approach on the natural sciences, seeking laws of cause and effect.

▶ Structured interviews enable them to test hypotheses by revealing correlations and possible cause-and-effect relationships.

Reliability

Structured interviews are a *standardised measuring instrument*. Pre-coded answers mean that a later researcher will categorise answers in the same way as the original researcher.

▶ As interviewees are asked exactly the same questions, we can compare their answers easily to identify similarities and differences.

Representativeness

Structured interviews are relatively quick and cheap, enabling larger numbers to be conducted.

▶ Positivists need representative data as a basis for making generalisations and cause-and-effect statements about the wider population.

▶ However, those willing to be interviewed may be untypical, resulting in unrepresentative findings.

Interpretivist criticisms

Interpretivists criticise SIs for their lack of validity:

▶ They give interviewers little freedom to explain questions or clarify misunderstandings.

▶ Structured interviews usually use closed-ended questions, forcing interviewees to choose from a limited number of pre-set answers.

▶ Interviewees may lie or exaggerate.

▶ The researcher has decided in advance what is important, which may not be what the *interviewee* thinks is important – thus imposing the researcher's ideas.

Feminist criticisms

Feminists argue that the relationship between interviewer and interviewee reflects the exploitative nature of patriarchal gender relationships.

▶ Oakley argues that this positivistic, 'masculine' approach to research values objectivity and regards 'science' as more important than the interests of the people it researches.

▶ Graham (1983) claims that SIs distort women's experiences because they impose the researcher's categories on women.

Interviews as social interactions

All interviews involve a social interaction, which may undermine validity.

▶ **Status differences** between interviewer and interviewee may affect honesty or willingness to cooperate.

▶ **Cultural differences** may lead to misunderstandings over meanings of words.

▶ **Social desirability:** interviewees may give false answers to make them seem more interesting.

▶ **Interviewer bias:** interviewers may ask 'leading' questions, influence answers by tone of voice, or identify too closely with interviewees.

▶ Though all interviews risk distorting the data, SIs may be less susceptible because the interaction is reduced, e.g. by following a fixed list of pre-set questions.

Analysis
Structured interviews are reliable because they are easy to standardise and control (e.g. the same questions, wording) and so are easily replicated.

Analysis
There is a better chance of obtaining a representative sample because of the relatively high response rates and sophisticated sampling techniques that are often used.

Interpretation
Link these criticisms to the positivist-interpretivist debate. Interpretivists seek to emphasise the need for validity to reveal actors' meanings, yet SIs do not allow us to access these meanings.

Unstructured interviews

Unstructured interviews have no standardised format and give the interviewer freedom to vary the interview. The result is rich, detailed qualitative data that gives an insight into the meanings and world of the interviewee.

Practical issues

▶ Their informality allows the interviewer to develop rapport and empathy, putting the interviewee at ease and encouraging them to open up.

▶ Training needs to be more thorough and interviewers need both sociological insight and good interpersonal skills to establish rapport.

▶ They take a long time – often several hours each. This reduces sample size.

▶ They produce large amounts of data, which takes time to transcribe. The absence of pre-coded answers makes analysis and categorisation of data difficult.

▶ They are very flexible, with no fixed set of questions. New hypotheses can be developed and tested as they arise during the interview.

▶ They are useful where the subject is one we know little about. Because they are open-ended and exploratory, they allow us to learn as we go along.

▶ Because there are no pre-set questions, they allow the interviewee more opportunity to speak about things that they think are important.

Theoretical issues: interpretivism

Interpretivists favour UIs because they produce valid data.

Involvement For interpretivists, understanding comes through involvement. By developing rapport, the researcher can see the world through the interviewee's eyes.

Grounded theory Interpretivists reject the positivist idea that research begins with a fixed, testable hypothesis. Instead, we should approach the research with an open mind to discover the truth.

Interviewees can raise issues, bringing fresh insights. The interviewer's probing helps interviewees focus their thoughts.

Open-ended questions permit interviewees to express themselves in their own words and reveal their true meanings.

Theoretical issues: positivism

Positivists reject UIs as unscientific, lacking objectivity, reliability and representativeness.

Reliability UIs are not reliable, because they are not a standardised measuring instrument.

Quantification Open-ended questions mean it is harder to categorise and quantify answers.

Representativeness Sample sizes are often very small, making it harder to make valid generalisations about the wider population.

Validity Interaction between interviewer and interviewee undermines validity.

Application

Developing rapport is particularly useful when researching sensitive topics; e.g. empathy enables interviewees to discuss sensitive subjects such as abuse.

Analysis

Their flexibility makes it much easier for both interviewer and interviewee to check they have understood and to clarify each other's meanings, leading to more accurate, valid data.

Application

Explain how characteristics of UIs meet the interpretivist concern to understand actors' meanings; e.g. open-ended questions allow for the open-mindedness needed for grounded theory.

Evaluation

Interpretivists see this as less of a problem because they do not emphasise generalisation. They are seeking actors' meanings, not causal laws.

ONE TO TRY

Question Assess the strengths and limitations of different types of interviews in sociological research.   (33 marks)

Examiner's Advice Consider different types of interviews and although your main focus should be on structured and unstructured interviews, you should make some reference to group interviews. Examine both strengths and limitations of interviews, in terms of practical, ethical and theoretical issues. Practical issues include cost, numbers covered, response rate, type of data required, flexibility/inflexibility etc. There are few ethical issues, though some feminists criticise SIs, while UIs may cause distress when dealing with sensitive issues. Theoretical aspects include reliability, representativeness, validity, objectivity, grounded theory etc. Put these into the broader context of positivism, interpretivism and feminism.

4 Observation

Key Issues

▶ What different observational methods do sociologists use?

▶ What are the practical, ethical and theoretical strengths and limitations of overt and covert participant observation?

▶ What is the usefulness of observation in relation to wider issues of methodological perspective, science, values and objectivity?

Types of observation

Non-participant observation (NPO) The researcher simply observes without taking part.

Participant observation (PO) The researcher observes while taking part in the group.

Overt observation The researcher's true identity and purpose are known to those being studied.

Covert observation The researcher conceals their true identity and purpose, usually posing as a member of the group.

Structured observation Observations are recorded using an observation schedule or checklist.

Most observation is unstructured PO used by interpretivists. Positivists sometimes use structured NPO.

> **Interpretation**
> If a question asks about 'observation', ensure you consider the full range of types of observation. Put your discussion in the context of the positivism-interpretivism debate.

Participant observation

With PO, researchers face problems of getting into, staying in and getting out of the group.

Getting in

▶ Some groups are easier to enter; e.g. joining a football crowd is easier than joining a criminal gang. Joining often depends on personal skills, pure chance, or the researcher's class, age, gender etc.

▶ The observer may have to overcome suspicions and win the group's trust, e.g. by befriending a key informant.

> **Analysis**
> The researcher needs a role that will permit them to make observations. This might conflict with the need to avoid disrupting the group's normal behaviour.

Staying in

▶ Once accepted, the researcher is faced with a dilemma: they must be involved in the group to understand it fully, yet they must also be detached from the group to remain objective.

▶ The longer the researcher spends in the group, the more chance they will cease to notice things that would earlier have struck them as noteworthy.

> **Analysis**
> This creates problems of validity. If the researcher is too detached, they fail to gain a true understanding; if they are too involved, they risk going native and becoming biased.

Getting out

Getting out of the group is generally less of a problem: the researcher can usually just leave.

▶ But if the research is conducted on and off over a period of time, there is a problem with making continual readjustments.

▶ Loyalty to the group may prevent the researcher from disclosing all they have learnt.

Practical issues in PO

There are other practical issues for the researcher who chooses to use PO.

Insight We gain insight into other people's lives by putting ourselves in their place – a process known as *verstehen*. This produces large amounts of rich, detailed qualitative data that give us a 'feel' for what it is like to be a member of the group.

Access PO may be the only method of studying certain groups, e.g. deviants may be suspicious of outsiders.

Flexibility PO is very flexible. Researchers enter the research with a relatively open mind and can formulate new hypotheses arising from their experiences.

Practical limitations Fieldwork is very time-consuming, sometimes taking years, and produces large amounts of qualitative data, which can be hard to analyse and categorise. The researcher needs training; observation can be stressful and sometimes dangerous. Powerful groups may be able to prevent sociologists participating.

Overt PO

The researcher:

▶ Can behave normally and opt out of dangerous activities.

▶ Needs no special knowledge or personal characteristics.

▶ Can ask naïve but important questions, take notes openly and use other methods to check observations.

▶ May be prevented by the group from entering.

▶ Risks creating the Hawthorne effect, undermining validity.

Covert PO

The researcher:

▶ Must maintain an act, which can be stressful and may need detailed knowledge of the group's way of life before joining. May have to engage in dangerous activities.

▶ May have no other way of obtaining data.

▶ Cannot ask naïve questions, has to rely on memory and write notes in secret, and cannot combine observation with overt methods.

▶ Doesn't risk altering the group's behaviour too much.

Application
Explain some of these limitations by applying them to examples from studies that have used PO.

Theoretical issues in PO

Interpretivism

Interpretivists favour PO because their key criterion is how far a method can produce valid data. They regard PO as producing a richly detailed, authentic picture of actors' meanings.

▶ **Validity through involvement** PO involves a high level of involvement with the group being studied. By experiencing the group's life first hand, the researcher gets close to people's lived reality, gaining a deep understanding of their meanings.

▶ **Flexibility and grounded theory** By starting without a pre-formed hypothesis or questions, researchers can modify their ideas in the course of the research to produce grounded theory: concepts and hypotheses grounded in the observed realities, rather than imposed by the researcher.

▶ By spending lengthy periods of time with a group, we are able to see actors' meanings as they develop.

Positivism

Positivists reject the use of PO as unscientific for several reasons:

Representativeness The group studied is often very small, selected haphazardly and unrepresentative.

▶ Thus, although PO may provide valid insights into the particular group, these *internally valid* insights are not necessarily *externally valid* (generalisable to the wider population).

Analysis
Compared with other methods, PO gives us a more dynamic picture than the 'snapshots' taken by interviews or questionnaires, and direct involvement allows us to see what people really do rather than what they say they do.

Evaluation
These characteristics make it very difficult to replicate the original study, so we cannot be confident that its findings are true.

Reliability PO is unsystematic and lacks reliability because it is not a standardised, scientific measuring instrument.

▶ The research depends heavily on the personal skills and characteristics of the lone researcher.

▶ Qualitative data from PO makes comparisons with other studies difficult.

Bias and lack of objectivity The researcher's deep involvement with the group results in a lack of objectivity and the danger of over-identifying with the group.

▶ The sociologist may conceal sensitive information.

▶ PO appeals to sociologists whose sympathies often lie with the underdog, such as interactionists.

▶ Positivists argue that findings from PO merely reflect the values and subjective impressions of the observer.

▶ From the large amount of data collected, the researcher must make judgments about what to omit from the final account, and this will reflect their values.

Evaluation
These characteristics undermine validity; e.g. by selecting what data to include, the researcher is merely giving their own view of things, not that of the actors.

Positivism and structured observation

When positivists use observational methods, they generally favour *structured non-participant observation*:

▶ It is quicker, so a larger, more representative sample can be studied.

▶ The observer remains detached: they do not 'go native' and lose objectivity.

▶ It uses standardised observational categories.

▶ However, interpretivists reject structured observation because it imposes the researcher's view of reality.

Analysis
These characteristics meet positivist criteria; e.g. standardised observational categories produce reliable, quantitative data, allowing researchers to establish causal relationships.

Ethics and observation

Covert PO raises serious ethical issues:

▶ It involves deceiving people in order to obtain information by pretending to be their friend.

▶ It is normally impossible to gain informed consent.

▶ Observers may have to lie about why they are leaving the group.

▶ They may have to participate in immoral or illegal acts as part of their 'cover'.

▶ PO leads to close personal attachments with the group, so the researcher risks over-identifying. This may result in condoning ethically unacceptable behaviour.

Interpretation
These ethical issues often conflict with practical advantages; e.g. avoiding the Hawthorne effect often involves deceiving people about the observer's true identity.

Structure versus action perspectives

PO is normally associated with 'action' perspectives, especially interactionism.

▶ **Interactionists** see society as constructed from the 'bottom up', through the face-to-face interactions of individual actors. PO is a valuable tool for examining these interactions.

▶ **Structural sociologists** (e.g. Marxists, functionalists) see this as ignoring the macro structural forces that shape behaviour, e.g. class inequality.

Interpretation
Link this to functionalist or Marxist concepts; e.g. Marxists argue that actors may suffer from false consciousness and misunderstand their true class position.

ONE TO TRY

Question Assess the usefulness of different types of observation in sociological research. (33 marks)

Examiner's Advice Begin by identifying the full range of types of observation that sociologists may use. Examine the practical, ethical and theoretical issues involved in using different types of observation, using examples from studies. Practical issues include time, cost, access, what role to adopt, danger, personal characteristics etc. Theoretical issues centre on validity, reliability and representativeness. Explain these terms and link them to PO and to the positivism-interpretivism debate. Distinguish between overt and covert PO. Although your main focus should be PO, examine structured non-PO as an alternative method favoured by positivists.

5 Official Statistics

Key Issues

▶ What are the practical, ethical and theoretical strengths and limitations of official statistics?

▶ How useful are official statistics in relation to wider issues of methodological and theoretical perspective, science, values and objectivity?

Official statistics are quantitative data created by the government or other official bodies, e.g. statistics on births, deaths, exam results, crime and the ten-yearly Census of the whole UK population.

▶ Governments use official statistics in policy-making.

▶ Official statistics are created by registration, official surveys and administrative records.

Various non-state organisations, e.g. churches and charities, also produce 'non-official' statistics.

Practical issues

Advantages

▶ Only the state has the resources to conduct expensive large-scale surveys and sociologists can access these for free to use in their research.

▶ Only the state has the power to compel individuals to supply certain data; e.g. parents are required by law to register births. This reduces the problem of non-response.

▶ Official statistics are collected at regular intervals showing trends and patterns.

Disadvantages

▶ There may be no statistics available on the topic the sociologist is interested in.

▶ The definitions the state uses may be different from the sociologist's.

▶ The state may change the definitions it uses, making comparisons over time difficult.

Theoretical issues: positivism

Positivists assume official statistics are reliable, objective social facts – a major source of representative, quantitative data that allows them to identify and measure behaviour patterns and trends.

▶ Statistics can be used to develop and test hypotheses, identify correlations and discover causal laws.

Representativeness

▶ Because they are very large-scale, some official statistics are extremely representative.

▶ Statistics from official surveys may be less representative because they are often only based on a *sample* of the relevant population. However, these surveys are still much bigger than most sociologists could afford to carry out.

▶ Great care is taken with sampling procedures to ensure representativeness when conducting official surveys.

Application

The Census covers the whole population and asks everyone the same questions, making it easy to compare different groups, regions etc.

Evaluation

The advantages and disadvantages both stem largely from statistics being secondary data. They are collected by official agencies, but for their own purposes.

Application

Use Durkheim's study of suicide to illustrate this. He correlated official statistics on suicide rates with those on religion to show a link between Protestantism and suicide.

Reliability

▶ Statistics from *official surveys*, e.g. the Census, are particularly reliable. These are carried out using a standardised measuring instrument administered in the same way to all respondents.

▶ Statistics from *registration data*, e.g. births and deaths, result from standard procedures – so any properly trained person will allocate a given case to the same category.

Theoretical issues: interpretivism

Interpretivists reject the positivist claim that official statistics are objective social facts – statistics are merely social *constructs*.

▶ For example, official statistics on mental illness are a record of the number of people that doctors decide are suffering from a mental illness.

▶ To end up as a statistic, the individual must go through a series of interactions with medical professionals, family etc.

▶ Interpretivists argue that the statistics do not show the 'real rate' of mental illness, but merely the decisions made by doctors to *label* people as mentally ill.

However, not all official statistics are equally invalid:

▶ **Soft statistics**, e.g. crime statistics, are less valid because they are often compiled from the decisions made by agencies such as police or courts. There is a 'dark figure' of unreported and/or unrecorded cases.

▶ **Hard statistics**, e.g. births and deaths, are much more valid; very few go unrecorded.

Marxism and statistics

Marxists also reject the positivist claim that official statistics are objective facts. They regard them as serving the interests of capitalism.

▶ Marxists see official statistics as performing an ideological function; e.g. politically sensitive data revealing the exploitative nature of capitalism may not be published.

▶ The definitions used in official statistics also conceal the reality of capitalism; e.g. the definition of unemployment has often been changed, thereby reducing official unemployment rates.

Feminism and statistics

▶ Many feminists reject the use of the quantitative survey methods that are often used to gather official statistics as a patriarchal model of research.

▶ Official statistics are created by the state, which maintains patriarchal oppression. They conceal or legitimate gender inequality; e.g. official statistics define full-time housewives as 'economically inactive'.

ONE TO TRY

Question 'Official statistics are socially constructed and reflect the interests of dominant social groups. As such, they are of little value to the sociologist.'

Assess the strengths and limitations of official statistics in sociological research.

(33 marks)

Examiner's Advice Usually an answer to a question on statistics might start by identifying their strengths and then their limitations. However, because the quote in the question takes a critical line, you could start with limitations instead. 'Socially constructed' prompts the interpretivist critique, which criticises the validity of official statistics – whereas 'interests of dominant groups' wants you to consider Marxist and feminist criticisms. You could then discuss positivist counter-claims relating to the theoretical advantages of statistics (e.g. reliability, representativeness) and their practical strengths (e.g. free, already collected).

6 Documents

Key Issues

▶ What are the practical, ethical and theoretical strengths and limitations of documents?
▶ How useful are documents in relation to wider issues of methodological perspective, science, values and objectivity?

Types of documents

Sociologists may use a variety of documents in their research, such as:

▶ **Written texts**, e.g. diaries, letters, e-mails, SMS texts, websites, novels, newspapers, school reports, government reports, medical records, parish registers, bank statements, graffiti.

▶ **Other texts**, e.g. paintings, drawings, photos, recorded or broadcast material from film, TV, music, radio, home video.

We can identify different types of documents:

Public documents from government departments, schools, welfare agencies, businesses, charities etc, e.g. Ofsted reports, council meeting minutes, media output, company accounts, records of parliamentary debates, reports of public enquiries.

Personal documents are first-person accounts of events and personal experiences, e.g. letters, diaries, photo albums, autobiographies.

Historical documents are personal or public documents created in the past.

> **Interpretation**
> If the question doesn't specify any particular type of document, make sure you differentiate throughout your answer between the different kinds.

Practical issues

▶ Documents may be the only source of information available, e.g. when studying the past.

▶ They are a quick and cheap source of large amounts of data. Someone else has already gathered or created the information.

▶ However, it is not always possible to gain access to them.

▶ Individuals and organisations create documents for their own purposes, not the sociologist's, so they may not answer the sociologist's questions.

> **Evaluation**
> Just because a source is cheap and easily accessed doesn't necessarily mean it is of great value to the sociologist – it may have too many other limitations.

Theoretical issues

Whether and how to use documents depends on the sociologist's methodological perspective.

▶ **Interpretivists** favour the use of documents because of their validity.

▶ **Positivists** tend to reject them as unreliable and unrepresentative.

Validity

Interpretivists believe documents give us a valid picture of actors' meanings; e.g. the rich qualitative data of diaries and letters give an insight into the writer's worldview.

▶ Thomas and Znaniecki's (1919) interactionist study of Polish migration and social change used a variety of documents: 764 letters, autobiographies, and public documents (newspaper articles, court and social work records).

▶ Because documents are not written with the sociologist in mind, they are more likely to be an authentic statement of their author's views.

> **Interpretation**
> However, positivists do sometimes carry out content analysis of documents as a way of producing quantitative data.

Application
You can apply examples of particular documents to illustrate these problems, e.g. the 'Hitler diaries' forgery.

However, a document may lack validity. Scott (1990) identifies three reasons for this:

Authenticity, e.g. a famous person's supposed diary may be a forgery.

Credibility Is it believable? It may lack credibility e.g. if written long after the events it describes.

Misinterpretation The sociologist may misinterpret what it meant to the writer and the intended audience. Different sociologists may interpret the same document differently.

Reliability

Positivists regard documents as unreliable sources, since they are often not standardised.

▶ Every person's diary is unique, even when each diarist is recording the same events.

▶ Uniqueness makes a document unrepresentative, so it is difficult to make generalisations.

Representativeness

Analysis
Not all documents survive; some official documents are covered by the Official Secrets Act; some private documents may never become available.

▶ Documents may be unrepresentative because some groups may not create them; e.g. the illiterate don't write letters.

▶ The evidence in documents that we have access to may not be typical of evidence in other documents that we don't have access to.

Ethics and documents

Application
You could apply an ethical defence of the use of leaked data if it can be justified as serving the public interest, e.g. if it revealed wrongdoing.

▶ Concerns about informed consent vary according to the type of document. Public documents are already in the public domain, so no consent is required.

▶ Where documents relating to the activities of public organisations have been 'leaked' to the researcher, informed consent obviously will not have been obtained.

▶ Obtaining informed consent to use private documents can be difficult. This may include both the author and anyone else referred to in the document.

▶ With historical documents, there is less concern if those involved are dead.

Content analysis

Content analysis is a method of analysing documents, e.g. news broadcasts, magazine stories, newspaper articles. There are two types: formal content analysis and thematic analysis.

Formal content analysis (FCA) produces quantitative data from qualitative content.

Evaluation
This may *not* be so objective. Drawing up the categories is a subjective process. Also, simply counting up how many times something appears in a document tells us nothing about its meaning.

▶ Usually a representative sample of material is selected. Then categories are decided on and used to code (i.e. classify) the coverage of the issue being investigated.

▶ FCA is attractive to positivists because they regard it as producing objective, representative, quantitative data from which generalisations can be made. It is also reliable.

Thematic analysis is a qualitative analysis of the content of media texts. It has been used by interpretivists and feminists. A small number of cases are selected for in-depth analysis. The aim is to reveal the underlying meanings 'encoded' in the documents.

ONE TO TRY

Question 'Lacking reliability and representativeness, personal and public documents are of little value to the sociologist.' Assess the strengths and limitations of personal and public documents in sociological research.   (33 marks)

Examiner's Advice The question refers to personal and public documents so make sure you differentiate between the two. It is also useful to refer to a range of examples of such documents. You should consider the practical, ethical and theoretical advantages and disadvantages of the different types of document. These include time, cost, scale, access, anonymity and confidentiality, representativeness and generalisation, hypothesis testing, reliability, validity and issues relating to content analysis. A useful way to organise your evaluation is by relating some of these to positivist versus interpretivist perspectives and quantitative versus qualitative data.

7 Methods in Context

Key Issues

▶ How can each method be applied to the investigation of particular research issues in crime and deviance?

▶ What are the strengths and limitations of each method for studying particular research issues in crime and deviance?

Using experiments to study crime and deviance

Application to crime and deviance

Sociologists sometimes use field experiments to study aspects of crime and deviance such as crime reduction strategies. The application of a specific crime reduction strategy to one particular area and not another enables the researcher to achieve a degree of control over the situation and develop an effective field experiment. Several researchers have also used laboratory experiments to investigate more general issues such as violence and obedience to authority.

Reliability

Although experiments in crime settings are unlikely to be exactly replicable, comparing areas or groups with broadly similar features allows experiments to be repeated in broadly similar ways, e.g. comparing the crime level in an area where a crime reduction strategy has been introduced with the level in an area where the strategy doesn't operate.

Ethical problems

Some experiments use people – offenders, victims and police – in real crime situations. However, there are particular ethical issues with carrying out experiments in these contexts. The experiment could affect a subject's chances of being a victim or of being rehabilitated. Crime is also a highly politicised issue and the researcher has no control over the political use of the research findings. Criminal and deviant acts are often more sensitive than other social actions, with many ethical concerns relating to violence, inter-personal relationships, becoming a victim etc. Laboratory experiments are rarely used in crime and deviance research for these reasons.

Limited application

Experiments are small-scale and can usually only examine a single aspect of behaviour. Larger issues in crime, such as the relationship between offending and social class, cannot easily be studied using this method.

Controlling all the variables

Experiments require researchers to control the variables in the situation. However, prisons, police forces etc are large, complex organisations, and many variables affect the behaviour of offenders, victims and law enforcement officers, e.g. age, class, crime contexts, type of prison. It would be impossible even to identify, let alone control, all the variables that might exert an influence.

Experiments have been used to study crime and deviance issues such as:

▶ **Inmates and prisons**

▶ **Aggression**

▶ **Obedience**

▶ **The effectiveness of crime prevention strategies.**

These issues can be examined in small-scale contexts that have physical or social boundaries.

Experiments are generally less useful for investigating crime and deviance issues such as:

▶ **Gender and offending**

▶ **The experiences of victims**

▶ **The functions of deviance.**

These issues are large-scale topics that are difficult or impossible to replicate in a laboratory or to find a suitable real-life situation to manipulate in a field experiment.

Using questionnaires to study crime and deviance

Questionnaires have been used to study crime and deviance issues such as:

▶ **Class and offending**
▶ **Attitudes to offenders**
▶ **Victims**
▶ **The effectiveness of crime prevention strategies.**

These are large-scale topics requiring a research method that can study large numbers of respondents relatively quickly and cheaply.

Practical issues

Questionnaires are very useful for gathering large quantities of basic information quickly and cheaply from large numbers of offenders, victims, police officers etc. Researchers can use questionnaires to correlate factors such as offending, victimisation or rehabilitation with variables such as age, type of punishment and gender.

Sampling frames

Although parts of the criminal justice system (CJS) have ready-made sampling frames, e.g. lists of police officers, these may not be available to the researcher because of the sensitivity of groups involved in law enforcement. There are few if any satisfactory sampling frames for criminals. Lists of prisoners comprise only those criminals convicted and jailed, not those who got away with their crimes or who were given non-custodial sentences.

Response rate

Response rates for questionnaires are often low. However, when conducted in prisons, response rates can be higher than in other contexts. Once a prison governor has put their authority behind the research, prison officers and inmates may be under pressure to cooperate. Police officers may also be accustomed to completing questionnaires issued in connection with their work.

Researching offenders

Offenders generally have below average literacy levels, so even a short questionnaire may be of only limited value as they may be unable or unwilling to complete it.

Representativeness

Obtaining a sampling frame from which to develop a representative sample is straightforward for some groups, e.g. police officers or prisoners, but less so for others such as victims of domestic violence. Response rates vary according to whose authority is behind the questionnaire and the groups it is sent to. For example, a questionnaire from the Bar Association to barristers is likely to produce a higher response rate than one sent to people involved in law-breaking.

Questionnaires are generally less useful for investigating crime and deviance issues such as:

▶ **Prison officer and inmate interaction**
▶ **Labelling**
▶ **Corporate crime.**

These issues involve more intense social interactions or powerful social groups, where giving out written questions to those involved after the event is unlikely to produce meaningful data.

Ethical issues

Some crimes are extremely sensitive, so although not having a researcher present may make it easier for victims or witnesses to respond, being handed a questionnaire to complete after a distressing experience is unlikely to create an empathetic situation.

Validity

Victim studies using questionnaires are retrospective and depend on respondents recalling often traumatic events. There is a greater possibility of distorted memory in relation to being the victim of crime than with other events.

Using structured interviews to study crime and deviance

Response rate

Structured interviews usually take less time than unstructured interviews and so they are less disruptive to the activities of the various CJS agencies. Therefore the research may be more likely to receive official support. The hierarchical nature of CJS agencies may then work in the researcher's favour and this may increase the response rate.

Structured interviews have been used to study crime and deviance issues such as:

▶ **Class and offending**

▶ **Fear of crime**

▶ **Attitudes to different crimes.**

These are large-scale issues requiring a research method that can investigate large numbers of respondents relatively quickly and cheaply.

Reliability

Structured interviews are easy to replicate. Therefore large-scale patterns in behavior can be identified, e.g. in gender and types of offending.

Validity

As young people tend to have better verbal than literacy skills, interviews may be more successful than written questionnaires as a method of obtaining valid answers from young offenders and victims. However, the formal nature of structured interviews may seem similar to experiences such as interviews with police. This may mean young offenders are less forthcoming.

Question design

It is more difficult to create questions for use with young offenders because their linguistic and intellectual skills are not fully developed. As a result, they may not understand some abstract concepts. They therefore need more help and clarification – which they are unlikely to receive in structured interviews.

Structured interviews are generally less useful for investigating crime and deviance issues such as:

▶ **Police-offender interaction**

▶ **Development of crime reduction policies.**

These issues are topics that require either direct observation or an examination of formal documents.

Power and status differences

There is a great deal of power and status inequality relating to crime and crime control. Prisoners may seek the approval of those in authority by giving untrue but socially acceptable answers, e.g. in the hope of winning privileges or early release. Researchers may be seen as authority figures, particularly in formal interview situations. This will reduce the validity of the interview data.

Sensitivity

Crime and deviance issues are generally more sensitive than most social issues, and the formal nature of structured interviews may be less appropriate. Victims of crime, witnesses, offenders, prisoners etc may all have experienced some degree of trauma that needs to be dealt with in a more sensitive manner than structured interviews allow.

Using unstructured interviews to study crime and deviance

Power and status inequality

Unstructured interviews may overcome barriers of power and status inequality. Their informality can establish rapport more easily, thereby encouraging interviewees to open up and respond more fully. This produces more valid data. This can be particularly useful when dealing with sensitive topics such as being the victim of violent crime, childhood abuse or racism within the CJS.

Unstructured interviews have been used to study crime and deviance issues such as:

▶ **The experience of imprisonment**

▶ **Street crime**

▶ **Racism within the CJS**

▶ **Victims of violent crime.**

These issues involve finding out the meanings and attitudes people hold, so in-depth, open-ended questioning is more appropriate.

Recording data

Those involved in crime and the CJS may be particularly unwilling to have their responses recorded on a digital recorder for fear of incriminating themselves. To an offender or police officer, recording by writing may also look too much like an official report is being written about them.

Safety

Research involving direct contact with certain violent offenders raises particular safety issues. Access may be limited, e.g. in prisons or police stations, because of safety concerns.

Access

There are particular problems in finding suitable interview venues. Criminals may be concerned about being seen talking to a researcher who may look like a police officer or journalist. Using the workplace or home may be inappropriate for interviewing whistleblowers within the CJS or the victims of domestic violence. There is little privacy in prisons for conducting sensitive interviews.

Validity

Some groups involved in crime or the CJS have their own language codes and unstructured interviews allow the researcher to stop and ask the meaning of specific language used. Few researchers have much personal experience of crime and the CJS, so the open-ended, exploratory nature of unstructured interviews allows the researcher to learn as they go.

Rapport

Given that offenders, police and others are likely to be defensive and suspicious, a higher level of trust is needed than with most social groups. Where there is a fear of possible punishment, getting to the truth below the surface is even more difficult and the more relaxed nature of unstructured interviews is helpful here.

Reliability

To put young offenders at ease, some interviewers try to maintain a relaxed atmosphere, e.g. by smiling, making eye contact etc. However, this cannot be standardised, so different interviewers may obtain different results, reducing the reliability of their findings.

Using observation to study crime and deviance

Access

Access may be very difficult, since many areas of the CJS are formally closed or strictly controlled by the power of the law. Criminals operate in relative secrecy to avoid detection and prosecution. Some aspects of the CJS, e.g. courts, are open to the public, giving an observer easy access.

Time

Crime and deviance do not always occur in a patterned and predictable way, so the observer can spend a long time simply hanging around waiting for relevant events to occur. Some settings, e.g. courts and prisons, are complex institutions and it can take time for the observer to become familiar with the system. The secretive and distrustful nature of criminal gangs means that becoming accepted can take a very long time. However, befriending a key member of the gang may speed up acceptance.

Personal characteristics

Observers may not share the social characteristics of those they study and this may limit research opportunities, or make those being observed suspicious and defensive.

'Going native'

Participant observation may lead to the observer over-identifying with those being studied. Punch observed police work and ended up acting like a police officer himself. Some observational studies of gangs, e.g. Venkatesh, have been criticised for romanticising gang culture.

Ethical issues

Covert observation of crime and policing involves major ethical issues, including participation in illegal activity. Venkatesh, observing overtly, acknowledged that he worked in ethically 'grey areas', knowing about the gang's law-breaking but not informing on them and participating to the extent the gang made him gang leader for a day. Who gains from observational research like this is also an ethical issue – those being studied, or researchers making a name for themselves?

The Hawthorne effect

Most observation has to be overt – there are few 'cover' roles the researcher can adopt because he or she stands out as being socially so different from those being observed. The Hawthorne effect is therefore often unavoidable because police officers, street gangs and others are likely to be suspicious of an outsider.

Unstructured interviews are generally less useful for investigating crime and deviance issues such as:

▶ **Social policies relating to crime**

▶ **Media representations of crime and deviance.**

These issues are either large-scale topics or they require detailed documentary analysis.

Observation has been used to study crime and deviance issues such as:

▶ **Delinquent subcultures**

▶ **Police and policing**

▶ **Court processes**

▶ **Minor crimes such as shoplifting.**

These issues can be examined in small-scale contexts and often involve observable social interaction.

Structured observation is generally less useful for investigating crime and deviance issues such as:

▶ **Corporate or green crime**

▶ **Social policy relating to crime**

▶ **Suicide.**

These issues are either large-scale topics or are difficult to observe.

Using official statistics to study crime and deviance

Official statistics have been used to study crime and deviance issues such as:

▶ **Levels of crime**

▶ **Patterns of offending**

▶ **Fear of crime.**

These issues are large-scale topics on which governments collect nationwide statistics.

Practical issues

The government collects a huge amount of statistical data on crime. Annual reports giving crime, judicial, prison and probation statistics as well as the British Crime Survey offer a huge resource to the sociologist. This saves sociologists time and money, and allows them to make comparisons, e.g. between offending rates for different classes, ethnic groups or genders.

Statistics also allow us to examine trends over time, e.g. in recorded offences, rates of imprisonment etc. Governments are interested in many of the same crime and deviance issues as sociologists so the statistics produced by government are likely to be very useful to researchers.

However, official definitions of key concepts may differ from those that sociologists use, e.g. social class.

Representativeness

Some official statistics on crime are highly representative; e.g. all police forces are required to maintain records of their activities. However, interpretivists argue that due to the social processes involved in crime and policing, there is a large 'dark figure' of unreported and unrecorded crime that undermines any claim to representativeness.

Official statistics are generally less useful for investigating crime and deviance issues such as:

▶ **Offender-police officer interaction**

▶ **Racist attitudes among prison officers**

▶ **Labelling.**

These issues are small-scale topics on which governments generally do not collect statistical data.

Reliability

The government uses standard definitions and categories in the collection of crime statistics. The same collection process is usually replicated from year to year, allowing direct comparisons to be made, e.g. of convictions. However, governments may change the definitions, categories and rules for recording offences. Where similar offences occur in the same incident, only the most serious one may be counted.

Validity

Interpretivists challenge the validity of crime statistics, seeing them as socially constructed, e.g. crime statistics are the outcome of interactions between police, suspects and others, based on labels and typifications, and influenced by policing policies, priorities and resources.

However, victim surveys and self-report studies may produce more valid statistics than those based on crimes known to the police.

Using documents to study crime and deviance

Practical issues

Because the CJS is run by the state and requires a large bureaucracy for it to function, an enormous amount of information about crime is created, some of which is publicly available. This includes policy statements, sentencing guidelines, minutes of meetings and working parties, legal documents, court records etc. Other documents include autobiographies of criminals, crime fiction etc.

Documents have been used to study crime and deviance issues such as:

▶ **Crime in the past**

▶ **Suicide**

▶ **State policy on crime.**

These issues require either a historical viewpoint, or the analysis of written or other texts.

Ethical issues

There are few ethical concerns with public documents produced by the CJS because they have been placed in the public domain. However, some sensitive material may not be made public.

There are more ethical problems with using personal documents such as suicide notes or diary entries and there is a greater need for anonymity because of potential consequences.

Reliability

Many CJS documents are in a systematic format, so researchers can draw direct comparisons. However, human errors made when completing these documents reduce their reliability.

Interpretation

Some crimes leave a documentary trail, e.g. fraud. However, this is sometimes very complex, requiring particular skills if the researcher is to unravel what has happened.

Representativeness

Because some documents are legally required of all elements in the CJS, the material produced is likely to be representative. However, the scale of this material makes it very time consuming to analyse. Personal documents produced by offenders or police officers are likely to be less representative.

Validity

Personal documents can provide important insights into the meanings held by those involved in the CJS and can therefore be high in validity. However, all documents are open to different interpretations. With some documents, there is also the problem of not knowing what the author has omitted, e.g. to avoid self-incrimination.

Documents are generally less useful for investigating crime and deviance issues such as:

▶ **Working-class experiences of crime**

▶ **Victim-offender interaction**

▶ **Labelling.**

These issues would require documents to have been created by those involved, which is unlikely to be the case.

Practice question and student answer

Item A

Researching the effectiveness of crime reduction strategies

Governments make crime reduction one of their main priorities. Sociologists disagree about which crime reduction strategies work best and they sometimes use field experiments to gauge the effectiveness of these strategies.

In a typical field experiment, the responsible government department will find two areas of the country that have very similar social characteristics and patterns of crime, and then apply a particular crime reduction strategy to one of these areas. For example, this might involve putting more police officers on the streets. After a period of time, the crime rates in the two areas will be measured. If the crime rate has fallen in the area where the crime reduction strategy has been put into practice, but not in the other area, then the strategy may be seen as successful.

However, it may be that crime has not actually fallen, but simply moved elsewhere. It is also difficult to identify all the variables in an area that might be relevant (such as social class, ethnicity, gender and age), let alone find two areas that are more or less identical in make-up.

Question

Using material from **Item A** and elsewhere, assess the strengths and limitations of using field experiments to study the effectiveness of crime reduction strategies.   (15 marks)

Student answer by Floyd

> There's not much point in identifying all the different types of experiments when the question specifies *field* experiments.

There are several forms that experiments can take: field, laboratory and comparative approaches. Each has its own strengths and limitations as a research method.

> Taking something from the Item, explaining it and linking it to the method in the question shows good Application skills.

As Item A suggests, governments often make crime reduction or prevention one of their main priorities. The importance of crime reduction means that governments are likely to put large amounts of public funding into assessing the effectiveness of crime reduction strategies. This means that there will be enough resources to carry out often long-term field experiments.

> This draws from the Item but doesn't take it much further – a missed opportunity to develop a useful point.

Experiments are generally favoured by positivists because they see the social world as having an objective reality that can be measured. By creating quantitative data, as field experiments do, researchers can see relationships between different factors, for example between crime reduction strategies and their effect on crime rates.

> Relevant point about lack of control, but it needs applying. At least identify some of the possible variables (e.g. population turnover, unemployment) and explain why they can't be controlled.

However, a field experiment does not have the same scientific credibility as a laboratory experiment. Not all the variables affecting outcomes can be identified or controlled. Many factors affect crime and the researcher has to take account of all of them in their field experiment. Some factors the researcher may not even be aware of. This problem affects the reliability of the experiment because it is not replicable.

> Ethics is an area you can explore, but everything here is true of any field experiment – it needs applying to crime reduction.

Field experiments may well have ethical problems. Researching without consent means researchers are breaching the British Sociological Association's code of practice. So does not allowing participants in the experiment the right to withdraw. Also, there is not likely to be much de-briefing of participants once the field experiment has finished. This is particularly a problem when studying criminal behaviour.

> Better – a good point appropriately applied. But it would benefit from some further development.

There are ethical problems with carrying out field experiments of this kind. In particular, when the issue is crime, with all the damage often associated with it, how ethical is it to try to reduce crime in one area but not in another and then stand by and watch what happens?

> A sound point, but it would be true of using field experiments to study virtually any issue.

There is also a problem with representativeness. Experiments are usually only carried out with a small number of people. A small sample, one geographical area, is unlikely to be representative of all the UK. Field experiments often can only study one aspect of behaviour at a time, in this case, one example of a crime reduction strategy.

> A potentially relevant theoretical reference, but it needs connecting to the specific issue of investigating crime reduction strategies.

Although interpretivists are highly critical of most field experiments, positivists value them highly because they see macro-sociological study as most important.

8/15

How to turn this into a top-mark answer

Floyd identifies a range of strengths and limitations of field experiments. Remember, though, that the key AO2 skill in 'methods in context' questions is Application, so it's essential to connect the strengths and limitations of the method to the specific issue in the question. In some paragraphs, Floyd does identify some relevant research characteristics of crime reduction strategies, but these are not very developed. In other paragraphs, he simply tells us about the method, not about its application to studying crime reduction strategies, or even crime in general.

Start from the characteristics of the research issue

By basing the answer on the method's strengths and limitations, Floyd then has to somehow find a way to attach research characteristics of crime reduction strategies to each of these. An alternative approach would be to start with the issue – the strategies – rather than the method, and attach strengths and limitations of the method to features of the issue. This is likely to be more effective.

For example, one characteristic of a crime reduction strategy is that many people in the area where it is being put into operation will know about it. This may create the Hawthorne effect and crime rates may change, not because of the strategy (i.e. the field experiment), but simply because people are aware that the experiment is taking place and change their behaviour as a result. For example, the public may be more likely to report crimes and the police may work harder to solve them. This will render the results of the experiment invalid.

Use the Item

It's important to take and develop as many points as you can from the Item. For example, it states that 'it may be that crime has not actually fallen, but simply moved elsewhere'. You could develop this by adding something like:

'The field experiment will then start to become very large because it will also have to investigate the surrounding areas for changes in their crime rates. Otherwise, there will be no way of knowing whether changes in crime in the experimental area are simply the result of it being displaced to neighbouring areas. This will increase the cost of the field experiment.'

Look for other clues and cues in the Item and see if you can link them to any strengths or limitations of field experiments that you know about.

CHAPTER 4 SOCIOLOGICAL THEORY

1 Functionalism

Key Issues
▶ What are the main features of the functionalist view of the social system?
▶ What is Merton's contribution to the development of functionalism?
▶ What are the strengths and limitations of the functionalist perspective on society?

Durkheim and functionalism

Interpretation
If the question asks about the functionalist perspective, include the work of Durkheim, Parsons and Merton, and examples from functionalist studies of different areas, e.g. education, crime, family, religion.

Durkheim was the most important forerunner of functionalism. He was concerned by rapid social change from a traditional society with a simple social structure to a complex modern society.

▶ **Traditional society** was based on *mechanical solidarity* with little division of labour, where its members were all fairly alike. A strong *collective conscience* bound them so tightly together that individuals in the modern sense did not really exist.

▶ **Modern society** has a complex division of labour, which promotes differences between groups and weakens social solidarity. Greater individual freedom must be regulated to prevent extreme egoism from destroying all social bonds.

▶ **Rapid change** undermines old norms without creating clear new ones, throwing people into a state of anomie (normlessness) that threatens social cohesion.

▶ **Social facts** Durkheim sees society as a separate entity existing over and above its members – a system of external social facts shaping their behaviour to serve society's needs.

Parsons: society as a system

Evaluation
An analogy is a way of understanding something by saying it is like something else – but it is not an explanation or proof of whatever claim is being made.

The organic analogy Functionalists see society as like a biological organism. Parsons identifies three similarities between society and an organism.

▶ **System** Both are self-regulating systems of inter-related, interdependent parts that fit together in fixed ways. In society, the parts are social institutions, individual roles etc.

▶ **System needs** Organisms have needs that must be met if they are to survive; e.g. society's members must be socialised if society is to continue.

▶ **Functions** The function of any part of a system is the contribution it makes to meeting the system's needs and thus ensuring its survival. For example, the circulatory system of the body carries nutrients to the tissues. Similarly, the economy meets society's need for food and shelter.

Value consensus and social order

Analysis
The central value system provides a framework that allows individuals to cooperate and social order to be maintained by ensuring that members of society agree on what they are aiming to achieve.

Parsons' central question is 'how social order is possible?' How are individuals able to cooperate harmoniously?

▶ Social order is achieved through a central value system or shared culture: a set of norms, values, beliefs and goals shared by members of a society.

▶ Parsons calls this *value consensus*. He sees it as the glue that holds society together.

Integration of the individual

Value consensus makes social order possible by integrating individuals into the social system and directing them towards meeting the system's needs.

▶ For Parsons, the system has two mechanisms for ensuring that individuals conform to shared norms and meet the system's needs:

1. **Socialisation** Through socialisation in the family, education, work etc, individuals internalise the system's norms and values so that society becomes part of their personality structure.

2. **Social control** Positive sanctions reward conformity, negative ones punish deviance.

▶ Socialisation and social control ensure that individuals are oriented towards pursuing society's shared goals and meeting its needs.

▶ By following social norms, each individual's behaviour will be relatively predictable and stable, enabling cooperation to occur.

Analysis
Socialisation and social control ensure that we each follow society's shared norms, and this enables others to predict our behaviour with confidence and so makes cooperation easier.

The parts of the social system

Parsons' model of the social system is like a series of building blocks:

▶ **Norms** At the bottom of the system specific norms or rules govern individuals' actions.

▶ **Status-roles** are 'clusters' or sets of norms that tell us how the occupant of a status (social position) must act; e.g. teachers must not show favouritism.

▶ **Institutions** are clusters of status-roles; e.g. the family is an institution made up of the related roles of mother, father, child etc.

▶ **Sub-systems** are groups of related institutions. For example, shops, farms, factories and banks form part of the economic sub-system.

▶ **The social system** These sub-systems together make up the social system as a whole.

Evaluation
Interpretivists argue that this *reifies* society, treating it as a real and distinct 'thing' over and above individuals, with its own needs – but only *individuals* have needs, not societies.

The system's needs: the AGIL schema

For functionalists, society is therefore a system with its own needs. But what exactly *are* the system's needs?

Parsons identifies four basic needs, summarised as 'AGIL' from their initial letters. Each need is met by a separate sub-system of institutions:

1. **Adaptation** of the environment to meet people's material needs (e.g. food, shelter). These are met by the *economic sub-system*.

2. **Goal attainment** Society needs to set goals and allocate resources to achieve them. This is the function of the *political sub-system*.

3. **Integration** The different parts of the system must be integrated together to pursue shared goals. This is performed by the *sub-system of religion, education and the media*.

4. **Latency** refers to processes that maintain society over time. The *kinship sub-system* provides 'pattern maintenance' and 'tension management', ensuring individuals are motivated to continue performing their roles.

Interpretation
Adaptation and goal attainment are *instrumental* needs, e.g. producing food to sustain the population. Integration and latency are *expressive* needs, since they involve emotions.

Types of society

Parsons identifies two types of society, each with its own typical *pattern variables* or sets of norms.

▶ **Traditional societies** with ascribed status. Relationships are broad and multi-purpose; norms are particularistic (treating different people differently); immediate gratification is emphasised; the group's interests come first – collective orientation.

▶ **Modern societies** with achieved status. Relationships are limited to specific purposes; norms are universalistic (same rules for everyone); deferred gratification is emphasised; individualistic orientation.

Analysis
Within each type, the variables 'fit' together; e.g. in modern society, students pursue their *individual* self-interest, *deferring gratification* to *achieve* status through education, with exams that judge everyone by the *same* standard etc.

Social change

Change is a gradual, evolutionary process of increasing complexity. Just like organisms, societies move from simple to complex structures.

▶ In traditional society, a single institution – kinship – performs many functions, e.g. providing political leadership, socialisation and religious functions.

▶ As society develops, the kinship system loses these functions, to factories, political parties, schools, churches etc.

▶ This is *structural differentiation* – a gradual process in which separate, functionally specialised institutions develop, each meeting a different need.

▶ Gradual change occurs through *moving (or dynamic) equilibrium:* as a change occurs in one part of the system, it produces compensatory changes in other parts.

Evaluation

Conflict theorists criticise functionalism for assuming that society is characterised by harmony and stability, and for failing to explain conflict and sudden change.

Analysis

A functional alternative – another institution that performs the same function; e.g. primary socialisation could be performed by lone-parent families or communes rather than nuclear families.

Merton's internal critique of functionalism

The functionalist Merton argues that Parsons is wrong to assume that society is always a smooth-running, well-integrated system. He criticises three key assumptions made by Parsons:

▶ **Indispensability** Parsons sees everything in society – family, religion etc – as functionally indispensable in its existing form. Merton argues that this is an untested assumption and that there may be 'functional alternatives'.

▶ **Functional unity** According to Parsons, all parts of society are tightly integrated into a single whole, so a change in one part affects all other parts. However, complex modern societies have many parts, some of which may be only distantly 'related' to one another and may have 'functional autonomy' (independence) from others.

▶ **Universal functionalism** For Parsons, everything in society performs a positive function for society as a whole. Yet some things (e.g. poverty) may be functional for some groups (e.g. the rich) and *dysfunctional* for others (e.g. the poor).

Manifest versus latent functions

Merton also makes a useful distinction between 'manifest' (intended) and 'latent' (unintended) functions.

Evaluation

The idea of dysfunction (negative function) draws attention to the possibility of conflicts of interest in society resulting from power inequalities that allow some groups to benefit at the expense of others.

▶ This distinction helps to reveal the hidden connections between social phenomena that the actors themselves may be unaware of.

▶ For example, the manifest function of the Hopi Indian rain dance was to cause rain, but the latent function was to promote solidarity during hardship caused by drought.

External critiques of functionalism

1 Logical criticisms

▶ **Teleology** is the idea that a thing exists because of its purpose or function. For example, functionalism claims that the family exists to socialise children – it explains the existence of the family in terms of its effect.

Evaluation

A real explanation must identify a *cause* – and logically, as a cause must come *before* its effect, we can't explain an institution's existence in terms of its effect.

▶ **Unfalsifiability** Functionalism is unscientific because its claims are not falsifiable by testing. For example, it sees deviance as both dysfunctional *and* functional – something which could never be disproved!

2 Conflict perspective criticisms

▶ Marxists argue that 'shared' values are not agreed but imposed on society in the interests of the dominant class.

▶ Conflict theorists see functionalism as a *conservative ideology* legitimating the status quo; e.g. assumptions of 'indispensability' help to justify the existing social order as inevitable and desirable.

Application
Explain how conflict and action criticisms link to the key ideas of perspectives such as Marxism and interactionism.

3 Action perspective criticisms

▶ Wrong criticises functionalism's 'over-socialised' or *deterministic* view of individuals in which they have no free will or choice – they are mere puppets whose strings are pulled by the social system.

4 Postmodernist criticisms

▶ Postmodernists argue that functionalism cannot account for the diversity and instability that exist in today's society.

▶ Functionalism is an example of a meta-narrative or 'big story' that attempts to create a model of the workings of society as a whole. Such an overall theory is no longer possible because today's society is increasingly fragmented.

ONE TO TRY

Question 'Functionalist theories are overly deterministic and ignore the extent of conflict and division in society.'

Assess the usefulness of functionalist contributions to our understanding of society. (33 marks)

Examiner's Advice Within your assessment of different functionalist contributions, you should keep a strong focus on the aspects identified in the question, that is, determinism, conflict and division. These are the criticisms made of functionalism by action, conflict and postmodernist approaches.

The standard approach to a question on functionalism might be to explain functionalist theories and then offer criticisms and alternatives put forward by other perspectives. This approach can be improved upon by tying in the criticisms from other perspectives to specific aspects of functionalism as you cover them (rather than in a separate section later on in your essay).

Furthermore, you should also try to point out some of the claimed strengths of functionalism – for example, that it is a complete theory of society, that it has a resonance today in New Right ideas and that it provides an analysis to underpin some approaches to social policy. You should use examples of functionalist analysis from areas that you are familiar with, e.g. crime and deviance, education, the family, religion etc.

2 Marxism

Key Issues

▶ What are Marx's main ideas and concepts?

▶ What are the differences between humanistic and structuralist Marxism?

▶ What are the strengths and limitations of Marxist approaches to the study of society?

Marx's ideas

Analysis
Marx differs from functionalists in not seeing progress as a smooth and gradual evolution but as a contradictory process in which capitalism would increase human misery before giving way to a classless communist society.

Interpretation
While Marx was the founder of the Marxist perspective, there have been many Marxists since, so in questions on this approach, make sure you deal with a range of different Marxist sociologists.

Analysis
The mode of production forms the *economic base* of society. This base determines all other features of society – the *superstructure* of institutions, ideas, beliefs and behaviour. This is the so-called *base-superstructure model* of society.

▶ Marxism is a perspective based on the ideas of Karl Marx (1818-83). Like Durkheim, Marx saw both the harm caused by modern industrial society and the promise of progress that it held.

▶ Like Durkheim, Marx believed that it was possible to understand society scientifically (he described his theory as 'scientific socialism') and that this knowledge would point the way to a better world. In these ways, Marxism is a continuation of the Enlightenment project.

▶ Marx was not just a theorist; he was also a revolutionary socialist and his ideas came to form the basis of communism. Marxism subsequently became the official doctrine of the former Soviet Union.

1 Historical materialism

▶ Materialism is the view that humans are beings with material needs, such as food and shelter, and must work to meet them using the *forces of production*.

▶ At first these forces are just unaided human labour, but over time people develop tools, machines etc. Humans also cooperate with one another, entering into *social relations of production* – ways of organising production.

▶ As the forces of production develop, the social relations of production also change. A division of labour develops that eventually becomes a division between two classes – a class that owns the means of production and a class of labourers.

▶ Production is then directed by the class of owners to meet their own needs. The forces and relations of production together are the *mode of production*.

2 Class society and exploitation

In the earliest stage of human history – *primitive communism* – everything is shared and there are no class divisions. But as the forces of production grow, different types of class society develop.

▶ In class societies, one class owns the means of production, enabling them to exploit the labour of others for their own benefit. In particular, they can control society's *surplus product* – the difference between what the labourers actually produce and what they need to subsist.

▶ Marx identifies three successive class societies:

1. **Ancient society**, based on the exploitation of slaves legally tied to their owners.

2. **Feudal society**, based on the exploitation of serfs legally tied to the land.

3. **Capitalist society**, based on the exploitation of free wage labourers.

3 Capitalism

Capitalism is based on the division between a class of owners, the *bourgeoisie* or capitalist class, and a class of labourers, the *proletariat* or working class. But unlike earlier class societies, capitalism has three distinctive features.

1. The proletariat are legally free and separated from the means of production. Thus, because they do not own any means of production, they have to sell their labour power to the bourgeoisie in return for wages.

2. Through competition, ownership of the means of production becomes *concentrated* in ever fewer hands; e.g. today's giant transnational corporations. This drives small independent producers into the ranks of the proletariat – they become *proletarianised*. Competition also forces capitalists to pay the lowest wages possible, causing the *immiseration* (impoverishment) of the proletariat.

3. Capitalism continually expands the forces of production in its pursuit of profit, production becomes concentrated in ever-larger units and technological advances de-skill the workforce.

▶ Concentration of ownership and the de-skilling of the proletariat together produce *class polarisation*. That is, society divides into a minority capitalist class and a majority working class who 'face each other as two warring camps'.

4 Class consciousness

Capitalism sows the seeds of its own destruction. Polarising the classes, bringing the proletariat together in ever larger numbers and driving down their wages means capitalism creates the conditions under which the working class can develop a consciousness.

▶ The proletariat then moves from being merely a *class in itself* to becoming a *class for itself*, whose members are class conscious – aware of the need to overthrow capitalism.

5 Ideology

The class that owns the means of material production (e.g. factories, land) also owns and controls the means of mental production – the production of ideas.

▶ The dominant ideas in society are therefore the ideas of the economically dominant class – spread by institutions such as religion, education and the media.

▶ However, as capitalism impoverishes the workers, they begin to see through capitalist ideology and develop class consciousness.

6 Alienation

Alienation is the result of our loss of control over our labour and its products and therefore our separation from our true creative nature.

▶ Under capitalism, alienation reaches its peak because workers are completely separated from and have no control over the forces of production, and because the division of labour is at its most intense.

7 The state, revolution and communism

The state exists to protect the interests of the class of owners who control it – the ruling class. The state is made up of 'armed bodies of men': the army, police, prisons, courts etc.

▶ Previous revolutions had always been one minority class overthrowing another, but the proletarian revolution that overthrows capitalism will be the first revolution by the majority against the minority.

▶ It will abolish the state, create a classless communist society, abolish exploitation, replace private ownership with social ownership, and end alienation.

Criticisms of Marx

1 Class

▶ Marx sees class as the only important division. Weber argues that *status and power* differences can also be important sources of inequality; e.g. a 'power elite' can rule without actually owning the means of production, as in the former Soviet Union.

▶ Marx's two-class model is simplistic. Weber sub-divides the proletariat into skilled and unskilled classes, and includes a white-collar middle class of office workers.

2 Economic determinism

▶ Marx's base-superstructure model is criticised for economic determinism. It fails to recognise that humans have free will and can bring about change through their conscious actions.

▶ Predictions of revolution in the most advanced capitalist countries, such as Western Europe, have not come true. It is only economically backward countries such as Russia in 1917 that have seen Marxist-led revolutions.

The 'two Marxisms'

The absence or failure of revolutions in the West has led many Marxists to reject the economic determinism of the base-superstructure model. They have sought to explain why capitalism has persisted and how it might be overthrown. Two models have emerged.

▶ **Humanistic or critical Marxism**, e.g. Gramsci, has some similarities with action theories and interpretive sociology.

▶ **Scientific or structuralist Marxism**, e.g. Althusser, is a structural approach with some similarities to positivist sociology.

Gramsci and hegemony

▶ Gramsci's concept of hegemony, or ideological and moral leadership, explains how the ruling class maintains its position.

▶ Gramsci sees the ruling class maintaining its dominance in two ways:

1. **coercion:** the army, police, prisons and courts of the capitalist state force other classes to accept its rule.

2. **consent (hegemony):** the ruling class use ideas and values to persuade the subordinate classes that their rule is legitimate.

However, ruling-class hegemony is never complete because:

▶ The ruling class are a minority and have to make ideological compromises with other classes.

▶ The proletariat have a *dual consciousness* – the poverty and exploitation they experience means they begin to 'see through' the dominant ideology.

▶ Gramsci rejects economic determinism as an explanation of change: even though economic factors such as mass unemployment may create the preconditions for a revolution, ideas are central to whether or not it will actually occur.

▶ Although ruling-class hegemony may be undermined by an economic crisis, this will only lead to revolution if the proletariat construct a *counter-hegemonic bloc* to win the leadership of society. The working class can only win this battle for ideas by producing its own *organic intellectuals*.

Althusser's structuralist Marxism

▶ For structuralist Marxists such as Althusser, it is not people's actions but social structures that shape history. The task of the sociologist is to reveal how these structures work.

▶ Althusser's version of Marxism rejects both economic determinism and humanism.

1 Criticisms of the base-superstructure model

Marx stated that society's economic base determines its superstructure of institutions, ideologies etc, and that contradictions in the base cause changes in the superstructure.

▶ Althusser's *structural determinism* is more complex. In his model, capitalist society has three structures or levels:

1. **The economic level**, comprising all those activities that involve producing something in order to satisfy a need.

2. **The political level**, comprising all forms of organisation.

3. **The ideological level**, involving the ways that people see themselves and their world.

2 Ideological and repressive state apparatuses

Although the economic level dominates in capitalism, the other two levels perform indispensable functions. *The state* performs political and ideological functions that ensure the reproduction (continuation) of capitalism.

▶ He divides the state into two 'apparatuses':

1. **The repressive state apparatuses (RSAs)** or 'armed bodies of men' that coerce the working class into complying with the will of the bourgeoisie. This is how Marxists have traditionally seen the state.

2. **The ideological state apparatuses (ISAs)** manipulate the working class into accepting capitalism as legitimate. This is a much wider definition of the state than the traditional Marxist view.

3 Althusser's criticisms of humanism

For structuralist Marxists, free will, choice and creativity are an illusion – everything is the product of underlying social structures.

▶ Humans are merely puppets and these unseen structures are the hidden puppet master, determining all our thoughts and actions.

▶ For Althusser, socialism will not come about because of a change in consciousness – as humanistic Marxists argue – but because of a crisis of capitalism resulting from what he calls *over-determination*: the contradictions in the three structures that occur relatively independently of each other.

Evaluation
While Althusser replaces economic determinism with a more complex 'structural determinism', this still leaves out human action and consciousness.

Application
Give examples of RSAs (army, police, prisons) and ISAs (media, education, family, reformist political parties, trade unions).

Interpretation
This is similar to Parsons' idea of status-roles, where society socialises individuals to slot into pre-existing roles that will meet the system's needs.

Evaluation
Marxists such as Gouldner and Thompson criticise Althusser for ignoring the fact that it is the active struggles of the working class that change society, not structural factors.

ONE TO TRY

Question Assess the view that Marxist theories are no longer relevant to our understanding of society. (33 marks)

Examiner's Advice The question asks about *theories*, plural. It is therefore important to go beyond traditional Marxism and to cover both the humanistic and structuralist versions of modern Marxism, such as Gramsci and Althusser. Start by explaining Marx's ideas and how the key concepts in his analysis, such as materialism, exploitation, class conflict, ideology, revolution etc, fit together. Evaluate his ideas as you cover each of them, both making criticisms, e.g. Weber's view that status and power are important as well as class, and pointing out the strengths. In your answer, focus on our understanding of society *today*. You can link the modern humanistic and structuralist versions of Marxism to the 'structure versus action' debate. You should also use examples of Marxist analysis from different areas of sociology that you are familiar with, e.g. in education, crime, religion, the family etc.

3 Feminist theories

Key Issues
▶ What are the main types of feminist theories?
▶ What are the similarities and differences between feminist theories?
▶ What are the strengths and limitations of feminist theories?

Types of feminism
▶ Feminism sees society as male dominated and it aims to describe, explain and change the position of women in society. It is both a theory of women's subordination and a political movement.

▶ A 'first wave' of feminism appeared in the late 19th century, with the suffragettes' campaign for the right to vote. The 1960s saw a 'second wave' emerge on a global scale.

▶ Since then, feminism has had a major influence on sociology. Feminists criticise mainstream sociology for being *malestream* – seeing society only from a male perspective.

▶ There are several feminist approaches, including liberal or reformist, radical, Marxist, dual systems, difference and poststructuralist feminism.

Liberal or reformist feminism

▶ **Liberalism** is concerned with the human and civil rights and freedoms of the individual, believing that all human beings should have equal rights.

▶ **Reformism** is the idea that progress towards equal rights can be achieved by gradual reforms in society, without the need for revolution.

▶ Liberal feminists (sometimes called reformist or 'equal rights' feminists) believe women can achieve gender equality through reform and promoting equal rights.

▶ Liberal feminists have documented the extent of gender inequality and discrimination, thus legitimising the demand for reform in areas such as equal pay and employment practices.

Cultural change
Liberal feminists also want cultural change because traditional prejudices and stereotypes about gender differences are a barrier to equality. For example, beliefs that women are less rational and more dominated by emotion are used to legitimate their exclusion from decision-making roles and their confinement to childrearing and housework.

Sex and gender
Liberal feminists distinguish between sex and gender:
▶ **Sex** refers to biological differences between males and females.
▶ **Gender** refers to culturally constructed differences between the 'masculine' and 'feminine' roles and identities assigned to males and females.
▶ While sex differences are seen as fixed, gender differences vary between cultures and over time. Thus, what is considered a proper role for women in one society or at one time may be disapproved of in another.

Interpretation
In answering questions on feminism, you need to explore a range of feminist approaches as well as the differences between feminism and other perspectives.

Application
Liberal feminists work for laws and policies against sex discrimination in employment and education. They believe this can secure equal opportunities for women.

Interpretation
Liberal feminism is a critique of the functionalist view of gender roles; e.g. Parsons distinguishes between instrumental roles (men's domain) and expressive roles (women's domain) and sees this distinction as biologically based.

Socialisation

Sexist attitudes and stereotypical beliefs about gender are culturally constructed and transmitted through socialisation.

▶ Therefore we must change society's socialisation patterns, e.g. promoting appropriate role models in education and the family, and challenging gender stereotyping in the media.

▶ Over time, liberal feminists believe, such actions will produce cultural change and gender equality will become the norm.

▶ Liberal feminism sees men and women as equally capable of performing the same roles; traditional gender roles prevent both men and women from leading fulfilling lives.

▶ This approach is the feminist theory that is closest to a consensus view of society – gender conflicts are not seen as inevitable and can be changed.

Evaluation
Marxist and radical feminists argue that liberal feminism fails to recognise the underlying causes of women's subordination and is naïve in believing that simply changing laws or attitudes will bring equality.

Radical feminism

Radical feminism emerged in the early 1970s. Its key concept is *patriarchy* – a society in which men dominate women.

▶ **Patriarchy is universal** Firestone argues that its origins lie in women's biological capacity to bear and care for infants, since performing this role means they become dependent on males.

▶ **Patriarchy is fundamental** It is the most basic form of social inequality and conflict: men are women's main enemy.

▶ **All men oppress all women** All men benefit from patriarchy, especially from women's unpaid domestic labour and from their sexual services.

▶ **Patriarchal oppression is direct and personal**, not just in the *public sphere* of work and politics, but in the *private sphere* of the family, domestic labour and sexual relationships.

Evaluation
Marxists argue that class, not patriarchy, is the primary form of inequality and that capitalism is the main cause and beneficiary of women's oppression, and not men, as radical feminism claims.

Sexual politics

Radical feminists argue that the personal is political:

▶ All relationships involve power and they are political when one individual tries to dominate another. Personal relationships between the sexes are therefore political because men dominate women through them.

▶ Radical feminists therefore focus on the ways in which patriarchal power is exercised through personal relationships, often through sexual or physical violence. For example, Brownmiller argues that fear of rape deters women from going out alone at night.

▶ **Sexuality** Malestream sociology regards sexuality as a natural biological urge and thus outside the scope of sociology. Radical feminists argue that patriarchy socially constructs sexuality so as to satisfy men's desires; e.g. the portrayal of women in pornography as passive sex objects.

Application
The idea that the personal is political emphasises the point that issues such as marriage, domestic labour, domestic violence, rape and pornography are about male *power*.

Women's liberation

Given that patriarchy and women's oppression are reproduced through personal and sexual relationships, these must be transformed if women are to be free.

▶ **Separatism** Some radical feminists advocate separatism – living apart from men and creating a new culture of female independence, free from patriarchy.

▶ **Consciousness-raising** Radical feminists argue for women-only consciousness-raising groups that may lead to collective action, e.g. 'reclaim the night' marches.

▶ **Political lesbianism** Some radical feminists argue that heterosexual relationships are 'sleeping with the enemy' and that lesbianism is the only non-oppressive form of sexuality.

Evaluation
Critics argue that vague utopian notions of separatism are unlikely to be achievable; e.g. heterosexual attraction makes it unlikely that the nuclear family will be replaced by single-sex households.

Marxist feminism

Marxist feminists see women's subordination as rooted in *capitalism*. Although individual men may benefit from women's subordination, the main beneficiary is capitalism.

▶ Women's subordination in capitalist society results from their primary role as unpaid homemaker, which places them in a dependent economic position in the family.

Functions for capitalism

Analysis
Explain how functions such as these serve capitalism; e.g. reproducing the labour force comes at no cost to capitalists; women's low pay holds down wage levels in general.

▶ **Reserve army of labour** Women are a source of cheap, exploitable labour for employers. They are a reserve army of labour – marginal workers who can be hired and fired to suit the needs of capitalism. They can be treated in this way because it is assumed their primary role is in the home.

▶ **Absorbing male workers' anger** This would otherwise be directed at capitalism.

▶ **Reproduction of labour** Women reproduce the labour force through their unpaid domestic labour.

Evaluation
The Marxist feminist claim that unpaid domestic labour benefits capitalism may be correct, but this doesn't explain why it is women and not men who perform it.

▶ Because of these links between women's subordination and capitalism, Marxist feminists argue that women's interests lie in the overthrow of capitalism.

Ideological factors

Some Marxist feminists argue that non-economic factors must also be taken into account if we are to understand and change women's position.

▶ **The ideology of familism** Barrett argues that we must give more emphasis to women's consciousness and motivations, and to the role of ideology in maintaining their oppression. In particular, the ideology of familism presents the nuclear family and its sexual division of labour (where women perform unpaid domestic work) as natural and normal. The family is portrayed as the only place where women can attain fulfilment.

Interpretation
Mitchell draws on Freudian psychoanalysis as well as Marxism to explain patriarchal oppression.

▶ Barrett believes that the overthrow of capitalism is necessary to secure women's liberation, but we must also overthrow the ideology of familism that underpins the conventional family and its unequal division of labour.

▶ **Femininity and the unconscious** Mitchell argues that ideas about femininity are so deeply implanted in women's unconscious minds that they are very difficult to dislodge and even after the overthrow of capitalism, it would still be hard to overcome deeply rooted patriarchal ideology.

Dual systems feminism

Dual systems feminists combine Marxist and radical feminism in a single theory. The two systems are:

▶ **Capitalism** – an economic system.

▶ **Patriarchy** – a sex-gender system.

▶ Dual systems theorists, e.g. Hartmann, see capitalism and patriarchy as two intertwined systems that form a single 'patriarchal capitalism'.

Evaluation
Some argue that patriarchy is not actually a system but merely a descriptive term for a range of practices such as male violence and control of women's labour.

▶ To understand women's subordination, we must look at the relationship between their position both in the domestic division of labour (patriarchy) and in paid work (capitalism), because the two systems reinforce each other.

▶ Walby argues that capitalism and patriarchy are inter-related, but that the interests of the two are not always the same:

  ▶ Capitalism demands cheap, exploitable female labour for its workforce.

  ▶ But patriarchy wants to keep women subordinated within the domestic sphere.

Difference feminism

Difference feminists do not see women as a single homogeneous group – differences of class, ethnicity, sexuality etc all lead to different experiences of patriarchy. Hence they emphasise diversity.

▶ Difference feminists argue that previous feminist theory has claimed a 'false universality' for itself: it claims to apply to all women, but in reality it is only about the experiences of white, western, heterosexual, middle-class women.

▶ **Essentialism** They claim that liberal, Marxist and radical feminists are essentialists. That is, they see all women as essentially the same. As a result, they fail to reflect the diversity of women's experiences and they exclude other women and their problems.

Interpretation
From this perspective, it is possible to see why many black feminists view the black family positively as a source of resistance against racism, rather than solely as a source of oppression.

Application
Women in poorer countries may see access to clean water and primary healthcare as more important than the concerns about sexual freedom that has been important to western feminists.

Poststructuralist feminism

Poststructuralism is concerned with discourses – ways of seeing, thinking or speaking about something. The world is made up of many, often competing, discourses, e.g. religious, scientific, medical and artistic.

▶ **Power to define** By enabling its users to define others in certain ways, a discourse gives power over those it defines; e.g. by defining childbirth as a medical condition and healthy women as patients, medical discourse empowers doctors and disempowers women.

▶ Poststructuralists argue that the Enlightenment project, with its talk of reason, humanity and progress, is simply a form of power/knowledge that legitimates the domination of western, white, middle-class males over other groups.

Anti-essentialism

Butler argues that the white, western, middle-class women who dominate the feminist movement have falsely claimed to represent 'universal womanhood' – but women are not a single entity who all share the same 'essence'.

▶ There is no fixed essence of what it is to be a woman, because identities are constituted through discourses and there are many different discourses in different times and cultures. For example, womanhood in Saudi Arabia is constituted partly by Islamic discourse, womanhood in the West by the discourses of advertising and the media.

Evaluation
Poststructuralist feminism abandons any notion of real, objective social structures affecting women's lives. Oppression is not just the result of discourses, it is about real inequality.

▶ Poststructuralism enables feminists to 'de-construct' (analyse) different discourses to reveal how they subordinate women, e.g. the medicalisation of childbirth.

ONE TO TRY

Question Assess the usefulness of different feminist approaches to our understanding of society today. (33 marks)

Examiner's Advice The question clearly refers to different feminist approaches so an answer needs to explore the differences – and the similarities – between feminist theories. Your answer should therefore explore liberal, radical, Marxist, dual systems and difference feminisms and the influence of poststructuralism. As well as exploring feminist theories it would be useful to refer to specific feminist studies or areas of particular research interest such as gender roles in the family or the role of political action. Another important area to explore is the way feminism has acted as a counter-balance to 'malestream' sociology.

4 Action Theories

Key Issues

▶ What are the differences between structural and action theories?

▶ What differences exist between the main types of action theory?

▶ What are the strengths and limitations of action theories?

▶ Action theories start from the opposite position to structural theories such as functionalism and Marxism. They are micro-level, 'bottom-up' approaches focusing on the actions and interactions of individuals.

▶ Action theories are more voluntaristic: individuals have free will and choice.

▶ The main action theories are social action theory, symbolic interactionism, phenomenology and ethnomethodology.

> **Interpretation**
> All four theories emphasise action, but they differ in how far they see structural explanations as valid, with the first two acknowledging some role for the social structure.

Max Weber: social action theory

Weber saw both structural and action approaches as necessary for understanding human behaviour, arguing that an adequate explanation involves two levels:

1. **The level of cause**, explaining the objective structural factors that shape behaviour.

2. **The level of meaning**, understanding the subjective meanings that individuals attach to their actions.

▶ In his study of the rise of capitalism, at the level of structural *cause*, the Protestant Reformation introduced a new belief system, Calvinism. This changed people's worldview, leading to changes in their behaviour.

▶ At the level of subjective *meaning*, work had a religious meaning for the Calvinists, as a calling by God. As a result, they accumulated wealth and became the first modern capitalists.

Types of action

Weber classifies actions into four types, based on their meaning for the actor:

1. **Instrumentally rational action**, where the actor calculates the most efficient means of achieving a given goal.

2. **Value-rational action** towards a goal that the actor regards as desirable for its own sake, e.g. worshipping god in order to get to heaven.

3. **Traditional action** is customary, routine or habitual action.

4. **Affectual action** expresses emotion, e.g. weeping out of grief.

> **Evaluation**
> Other action theorists argue that Weber's view of action is too individualistic and cannot explain the *shared* nature of meanings.

Symbolic interactionism

Symbolic interactionism focuses on how we create the social world through our interactions. These interactions are based on the *meanings* we give to situations, conveyed through *symbols*, especially language.

G.H. Mead

1 Symbols versus instincts

Unlike animals whose behaviour is governed by instincts, we respond to the world by giving meanings to the things that are significant to us. We create a world of meanings by attaching *symbols* to the things around us.

▶ Therefore there is an *interpretive phase* between a stimulus and our response to it, in which we interpret its meaning.

2 Taking the role of the other

We interpret other people's meaning by taking their role, i.e. putting ourselves in their place, seeing ourselves as they see us.

▶ This ability develops through interaction. Young children internalise *significant others* such as parents, while later in life we see ourselves from the point of view of society in general – the *generalised other*.

Herbert Blumer

Blumer identified three key principles of interactionism:

1. Our actions are based on the meanings we give to situations, people etc. They are not automatic responses to stimuli.

2. These meanings arise from interactions and are to some extent negotiable and changeable.

3. The meanings we give to situations are mainly the result of taking the role of the other.

▶ Blumer argues that although our action is *partly* predictable because we internalise the expectations of others, there is always some room for choice in how we perform our roles.

Labelling theory

Labelling theorists use three key interactionist concepts:

1. **Definition of the situation** Defining something labels it. Thomas argues that if people define a situation as real, it will have real consequences: if we believe something to be true, this will affect how we act and in turn may affect those involved.

2. **Looking-glass self** Cooley argues that our *self-concept* arises out of our ability to take the role of the other. Others act as a looking-glass to us: we see our self mirrored in how they respond to us and we become what they see us as.

3. **Career** Becker and Lemert apply this concept, e.g. to mental patients. The individual has a career running from 'pre-patient' with certain symptoms, through labelling by a psychiatrist, to hospital in-patient, to discharge etc. 'Mental patient' may become our *master status*.

Goffman's dramaturgical model

Whereas labelling theory sees the individual as the passive victim of other people's labels, Goffman describes how we actively construct our 'self' by manipulating other people's impressions of us.

▶ This is a dramaturgical approach: it uses analogies with drama, e.g. 'actors', 'scripts', 'props', 'backstage' etc.

1 Presentation of self and impression management

Two key dramaturgical concepts are the *presentation of self* and *impression management* – we seek to present a particular image to our audiences, controlling the impression our 'performance' gives.

▶ Impression management techniques include tone of voice, gestures, props and settings such as dress, make-up, equipment, décor and premises.

▶ As in the theatre, there is a 'front' stage where we act out our roles, while backstage, we can step out of our role and 'be ourselves', e.g. teachers' behaviour in the classroom and staffroom.

2 Roles

There is a 'gap' or *role distance* between our real self and our roles, which are only loosely scripted by society and allow us a lot of freedom in how we play them.

▶ Role distance implies that we do not always believe in the roles we play. We may be calculating, manipulating audiences into accepting an impression that conceals our true self.

Phenomenology

In philosophy, the term 'phenomenon' describes things as they appear to our senses. Some philosophers argue that we can never have definite knowledge of what the world outside is really like; all we can know is what our mind tells us about it.

Schutz's phenomenological sociology

Schutz applies this idea to the social world. We share the categories that we use to classify the world with other members of society.

▶ He calls these shared categories *typifications*. These enable us to organise our experiences into a shared world of meaning.

▶ The meaning of an action varies according to its social context. Meaning is given by the context, not by the action itself, so meanings are potentially unclear and unstable.

▶ Fortunately, typifications make social order possible, because they give members of society a shared 'life world' of commonsense knowledge that we can use to make sense of our experience.

▶ Schutz calls this 'recipe knowledge': like a recipe, we can follow it without thinking too much, using it to make sense of the everyday world.

▶ The social world is an inter-subjective one that can only exist when we share the same meanings.

▶ The fact that society *appears* to us as a real, objective thing outside of us simply shows that all members of society share the same meanings. In turn, this allows us to cooperate and achieve goals.

Ethnomethodology

Ethnomethodology also rejects the idea of society as a real objective structure 'out there'.

▶ Garfinkel argues that social order is created from the 'bottom up'. It is something members of society actively construct in everyday life using their commonsense knowledge.

▶ The sociologist's task is thus to uncover the taken-for-granted rules people use to construct social reality.

▶ **Indexicality** refers to the fact that meanings are always potentially unclear. This is a threat to social order, because if meanings are unclear or unstable, communication and cooperation becomes difficult and social relationships will break down.

▶ **Reflexivity** is the use of our commonsense knowledge to construct a sense of meaning and order, and so prevent indexicality occurring.

▶ Language is of vital importance in achieving reflexivity. It gives us a sense of reality existing 'out there', although in fact all we have done is to construct a set of shared meanings.

▶ Garfinkel used *breaching experiments* to disrupt people's expectations of a situation (e.g. students behaving like lodgers in their parents' home).

▶ These show how the orderliness of everyday situations is not inevitable and how we use our commonsense, taken-for-granted assumptions to actively *create* social order.

Combining structure and action

▶ **Action theories** are micro-level, voluntaristic theories that see society as inter-subjective, constructed through interaction and meaning

▶ **Structural theories** by contrast are macro-level, deterministic theories that see society as objective and external to individuals.

Giddens' structuration theory

Giddens seeks to combine the two approaches into a single unified theory of structure and action.

▶ He argues that there is a *duality of structure*. Structure and agency (i.e. action) are two sides of the same coin; neither can exist without the other:

▶ Our actions produce, reproduce and change structures over time and space, while these structures are what make our actions possible in the first place.

▶ Giddens calls this relationship *structuration*.

Reproducing structures through agency

For Giddens, structure has two elements:

▶ **Rules** The norms, customs and laws that govern action.

▶ **Resources** both economic resources and power over others.

▶ Rules and resources can be either reproduced or changed through human action. However, our actions generally tend to *reproduce* rather than change them. This is because society's rules contain a stock of knowledge about how to live our lives, so our routine activities tend to reproduce the existing structure of society.

▶ We also reproduce existing structures because we have a deep-seated need for *ontological security* – a need to feel that the world is orderly, stable and predictable.

Changing structures through agency

Change can happen because:

1. We 'reflexively monitor' (reflect upon) our actions and we can deliberately choose a new course of action. In late modern society, where tradition no longer dictates action, this is even more likely.

2. Our actions may have unintended consequences, producing changes that were not part of our goal.

> **Evaluation**
> Structuration theory is criticised for not really being a theory at all: it doesn't *explain* what happens in society; it just *describes* the kinds of things we will find when we study society.

> **Application**
> This can be applied to language. It is a structure with rules that make it possible for us to communicate, but our use of it can also change its structure, e.g. by giving words new meanings.

> **Evaluation**
> Giddens' claim that actors can change structures underestimates the capacity of structures to resist change; e.g. slaves may wish to abolish the institution of slavery, but lack the power to do so.

ONE TO TRY

> **Question** Assess the contribution of different 'action' theories to our understanding of society today. (33 marks)
>
> **Examiner's Advice** You should begin by explaining what is meant by 'action' theories, contrasting them with structural approaches. You need to use the appropriate terminology: determinism versus voluntarism, 'top-down' versus 'bottom-up', macro versus micro, objective versus subjective etc. You should refer to all four major theories: social action theory, interactionism, phenomenology and ethnomethodology. However, it is reasonable to focus on one – probably interactionism, ensuring you deal with both labelling theory and Goffman. Refer to the differences between action approaches, especially in relation to how far they give some role to structural factors. A useful way to end is to briefly discuss Giddens' structuration theory – does it bring action and structuralist approaches together or is it a weak compromise?

5 Globalisation, modernity and postmodernity

Key Issues
▶ What are the reasons for the trend towards globalisation?
▶ What is the difference between modernity, postmodernity and late modernity?
▶ What are the strengths and limitations of different theories of recent changes in society?

Modernity and globalisation

The Enlightenment project
Modernist theories (e.g. Marxism) are part of the Enlightenment project – the idea that through reason and science, we can discover true knowledge and progress to a better society.

The characteristics of modern society
Modern society emerged from the late 18th century. Its characteristics include the nation-state; capitalism; mass production; scientific thinking; technology; individualism and the decline of tradition.

Globalisation
Globalisation – the growing interconnectedness of societies – is occurring for several reasons:

▶ **Technological changes**, e.g. the internet and air travel create *time-space compression*.

▶ **Economic changes** Global networks dominate economic activity. The growth in transnational companies (TNCs) drives globalisation forward.

▶ **Political changes** The fall of communism and the growth of transnational bodies have created opportunities for global capitalism.

▶ **Changes in culture and identity** Westernised *global culture* makes it harder for cultures to exist in isolation. Globalisation undermines traditional sources of *identity*.

Explaining the changes
Rapid changes linked to globalisation have led to new questions:

▶ *What kind of society* do we now live in – modern society, or a new, postmodern society?

▶ *What kind of theory* can explain today's society – postmodernism, or some version of modernism?

▶ *The Enlightenment project* – can we achieve true knowledge to improve society?

Three theories offer answers to these questions: postmodernism; theories of late modernity; Marxist theories of postmodernity.

Postmodernism

For postmodernists, we now live in a new era: postmodernity. Postmodern society is a fundamental break with modernity and requires a new kind of theory to explain it.

Interpretation
In explaining the nature of modern society, show how some of these features link together, e.g. how science and technology are vital to the development of mass production.

Application
Link these economic changes to Beck's idea of 'global risk society'; e.g. the financial crisis that began in the USA in 2008 had global repercussions.

Analysis
Economic integration also encourages a global culture; e.g. TNCs selling the same consumer goods in many countries help to promote similar tastes across national borders.

Knowledge

Postmodernists argue that there are no objective criteria to prove whether a theory is true.

Analysis
Postmodernists take the relativist position that all views are true for those who hold them. No one has special access to the truth – including sociologists.

▶ Therefore any theory claiming to have the truth about how to create a better society, e.g. Marxism, is a mere *meta-narrative* – just someone's *version* of reality.

▶ We should celebrate the diversity of views rather than seek to impose one version of the truth.

The Enlightenment project

▶ In postmodern society, the media create *hyper-reality* – the media's signs appear more real than reality itself, leaving us unable to distinguish image from reality.

▶ If we cannot even grasp reality, we have lost the power to change it to improve society – the Enlightenment project is unachievable.

Culture and identity

▶ The media produce an endless stream of images, making culture unstable and fragmented; there is no longer a coherent set of shared values. People cease to believe any one version of the truth.

▶ Identity becomes destabilised: we can change it simply by changing our consumption patterns, picking and mixing media-produced images to define ourselves.

Criticisms of postmodernism

Application
Applying postmodernism's relativism to postmodernism itself reveals a logical flaw in the theory: it claims that no theory is any truer than any other – so why should we believe *its* claims are true?

▶ It ignores the ruling class' use of the media as a tool of ideological domination.

▶ It is wrong to claim people cannot distinguish between reality and media image.

▶ By assuming all views are equally true, it becomes just as valid to deny the Nazis murdered millions as to affirm it.

▶ Critics argue that we *can* use knowledge to solve human problems.

Theories of late modernity

Unlike postmodernism, theories of late modernity (TLM) argue that today's rapid changes are not the dawn of a new, postmodern era, but a *continuation* of modern society.

▶ We are now in *late* or *high* modernity. Key features of modernity have now become intensified; e.g. change has always been typical of modern society, but now it has gone into overdrive.

▶ Unlike postmodernism, TLM subscribe to the Enlightenment project.

Giddens: reflexivity and high modernity

High modernity has two key features that encourage globalisation and rapid change:

Disembedding is 'the lifting out of social relations from local contexts of interaction'. Factors such as credit break down geographical barriers and make interaction more impersonal.

Reflexivity Tradition and custom no longer serve as a guide to how we should act.

▶ We are thus forced to become *reflexive* – to reflect on and modify our actions in the light of information about risks.

▶ This means we are continually re-evaluating our ideas. Under these conditions, culture becomes increasingly unstable.

Late modernity and risk

▶ We now face new *high consequence risks*, e.g. environmental harm. Beck calls these 'manufactured risks' as they result from technology, not nature.

▶ However, unlike postmodernists, Giddens and Beck believe we can make rational plans based on objective knowledge to reduce these risks and achieve progress.

Marxist theories of postmodernity

Like Beck and Giddens, but unlike postmodernists, Marxists Jameson (1984) and Harvey (1989) believe in the Enlightenment project of achieving objective knowledge to improve society.

▶ However, they agree with postmodernists that we have moved from modernity to postmodernity.

▶ But rather than see this as a new type of society, Marxists see it as merely the most recent stage of capitalism.

Flexible accumulation

▶ Postmodernity arose out of the capitalist crisis of the 1970s, which gave rise to a new way of achieving profitability, which Harvey calls 'flexible accumulation' (FA).

▶ FA involves the use of ICT, an expanded service and finance sector, job insecurity and working 'flexibly' to fit employers' needs. It involves production of customised products for 'niche' markets and brings many of the features of postmodernity:

▶ Customised products promote cultural diversity.

▶ Leisure, culture and identity become commodities produced for profit.

▶ Global financial markets and ICT produce compression of time and space.

▶ It brings political changes, especially the weakening of the working-class movement. In its place, a variety of oppositional movements emerge, e.g. feminism, environmentalism.

ONE TO TRY

Question Assess the usefulness of postmodernism to our understanding of society today. (33 marks)

Examiner's Advice You can start by outlining some of the main features of today's society, e.g. by focusing on the impact of globalisation. You should then give an account of postmodernism, using key concepts such as meta-narratives, media-saturated society, hyper-reality, identity, consumption, diversity, instability etc. Examine the criticisms made of postmodernism, e.g. in terms of its pessimism towards the Enlightenment project, its logical flaws, its ignoring of power and inequality etc. Use theories of late modernity and Marxist theories of postmodernity as more plausible sociological alternatives to the postmodernist view of today's society.

6 Objectivity and values in sociology

Key Issues

▶ What do objectivity, subjectivity and value freedom mean?

▶ What are the main views of the relationship between sociology and values?

▶ Can and should sociology be value-free?

Values and sociology

All members of society – including sociologists – have values, beliefs and opinions.

▶ Some argue that it is both possible and desirable for sociologists to keep their subjective values out of their research.

▶ Others argue that staying value-neutral is impossible, because sociologists are humans studying other humans.

▶ Some argue that it is desirable for sociologists to use their values to improve society.

Interpretation
Read the question carefully: does it ask whether sociology *can* be value-free, *should* be value-free, or *both*?

The classical sociologists and values

▶ For the early positivists Comte and Durkheim, sociology's job was to discover the truth about how society worked and to improve human life.

▶ Sociologists would be able to say with scientific certainty what was best for society.

▶ Marx too saw himself as a scientist. He believed he had discovered the truth about society's future and the inevitability of classless society.

Analysis
This shows that Marx took for granted the value of communism as the ideal society and saw his scientific approach as helping to bring this society about.

Max Weber

Weber distinguishes between value judgments and facts. He argues that a value can neither be proved nor disproved by the facts – they belong to different realms. However, he still sees an essential role for values in sociological research:

1. **Values as a guide to research** We can only select areas of study in terms of their *value relevance* to us.

2. **Data collection and hypothesis testing** Sociologists must be as objective as possible when actually collecting the facts, e.g. not asking leading questions, and the hypothesis must stand or fall solely on whether or not it fits the observed facts.

3. **Values in the interpretation of data** Facts need to be set in a theoretical framework to understand their significance. This is influenced by the sociologist's values, which must therefore be stated explicitly.

4. **Values and the sociologist as a citizen** Scientists and sociologists are also citizens. They cannot dodge the moral issues their work raises or the uses it is put to by hiding behind 'value freedom'.

Application
Use the example of feminist research: feminists value gender equality, which leads them to study areas such as women's oppression.

▶ Weber thus sees values as relevant when choosing what to research, when interpreting data and in the use the findings are put to – but they must be kept out of the actual process of gathering data.

▶ Sociology cannot tell us what values or goals we should hold.

▶ But it *can* tell us what means we should adopt if we want to achieve certain goals that we value, and the consequences of holding those values.

Application
For example, we may hold the value that racial discrimination is a good thing, but sociology may tell us that this makes the economy less efficient by preventing some talented individuals from taking on important jobs.

Value freedom and commitment

20th century positivists

20th century positivists argued that their own values were irrelevant to their research because science is concerned with matters of fact, not value, so sociologists should remain morally neutral.

▶ Gouldner argues that by the 1950s, American sociologists in particular had become mere 'spiritless technicians' hiring themselves out to organisations such as government and the military.

▶ For Gouldner, they were dodging the moral issues that their work raised, e.g. in helping to prevent revolutions in South America.

Committed sociology

Myrdal and Gouldner argue that sociologists should not only identify their values. They should also openly 'take sides', espousing the interests of actual groups.

▶ It is undesirable to be value-neutral since, without values to guide research, sociologists are merely putting their services up for sale.

Whose side are we on?

The interactionist Becker asks: if all sociology is influenced by values, 'Whose side are we on?'

▶ Traditionally functionalists and positivists have taken the viewpoint of the *powerful*: police, psychiatrists etc.

▶ Becker argues that we should take the side of the *underdog*: criminals, mental patients etc.

▶ Identifying with the powerless links to the methods interactionists favour, e.g. PO, which they see as revealing the meanings of these 'outsiders'.

▶ Gouldner adopts a Marxist perspective, arguing that it is not enough to describe the underdog's life – sociologists should be committed to ending their oppression.

▶ According to Gouldner, we should not be celebrating 'the man on his back'; we should be supporting 'the man fighting back'.

Funding and careers

Most research is funded by government, businesses etc, and who pays for research may control its direction and the questions it asks.

▶ Funding bodies may prevent publication of the research if its findings prove unacceptable.

▶ Sociologists may want to further their careers. This may influence their choice of topic.

▶ They may censor themselves for fear of harming their career.

Values, perspectives and methods

For Gouldner, all research is inevitably influenced by values.

▶ Values influence the topics that sociologists of different perspectives choose, the concepts they develop and the conclusions they reach.

▶ Sociologists' values influence choice of methods; e.g. Becker's support for the underdog leads him to choose qualitative methods to reveal the underdog's world.

Application
Apply examples of the use of social science to assist military operations, e.g. Project Camelot in South America and Human Terrain System in Afghanistan, to illustrate the values involved in this work.

Evaluation
Gouldner criticises Becker for romanticising underdogs – the misunderstood, negatively labelled, 'exotic specimens' of deviant behaviour.

Analysis
Explain the link between perspectives and methods; e.g. functionalists make uncritical use of official statistics because they tend to take the side of the 'establishment'.

Objectivity and relativism

If all perspectives involve values, are their findings just a reflection of their values, not objective facts? Relativism argues that:

▶ Different groups and individuals have different views as to what is true and these reflect their own values and interests.

▶ There is no way of judging whether any view is truer than any other.

Relativism and postmodernism

▶ Postmodernists take a relativist view – there are no 'privileged accounts' of society that have special access to the truth.

▶ From a relativist standpoint, there is no single absolute or objective truth. What you believe to be true, *is* true – for you.

▶ Any perspective claiming to have the truth is just a meta-narrative or 'big story' based on values and assumptions.

Evaluation

Critics argue that postmodernism is itself a meta-narrative about what society is like – and so we shouldn't believe what postmodernism says either!

ONE TO TRY

Question Assess different sociological views of the role of objectivity and values in sociological research. (33 marks)

Examiner's Advice Start by identifying the two key questions of whether it is *possible* to keep values out of sociological research and thus be objective, and whether it is *desirable* to do so. Your answer should explore each of these questions, focusing on the positions taken by the classical sociologists (Comte, Durkheim, Marx and Weber), interactionists, Marxists such as Gouldner, and postmodernists.

Evaluate each as you examine their arguments. Use relevant examples, e.g. of perspectives or funding bodies influencing choice of topic or method, case studies (e.g. Project Camelot) etc.

7 Sociology and science

Key Issues

▶ How do positivists and interpretivists differ about whether sociology can be a science?

▶ What are the different views of natural science and what are their implications for sociology as a science?

▶ What are the arguments for and against the view that sociology can or should be a science?

Interpretation
Link these debates to the importance of science in the Enlightenment project and the influence of science on 19th century modernist sociologists, e.g. Durkheim and Marx.

There are two related debates:

▶ Can and should sociology be a science?

▶ What is (natural) science, and what implications does this have for sociology?

Positivism

Positivists believe it is possible and desirable to apply the logic and methods of the natural sciences to the study of society, to solve social problems and achieve progress.

▶ Reality exists outside and independently of the human mind so, like the natural world, society too is an objective factual reality.

▶ Reality is patterned, and these empirical (factual) patterns or regularities can be studied through systematic observation and measurement.

Evaluation
Interpretivists criticise positivists' attempts to uncover macro or structural causes of social phenomena for ignoring the role played by consciousness, meaning and choice.

▶ From this, sociologists can discover the laws that determine how society works, by using inductive reasoning verified through research evidence.

▶ Positivists aim to produce scientific laws about how society works in order to predict future events and to guide social policies.

Positivist methods

Positivists believe sociology should take the natural science experimental method as the model for research because the investigator can test a hypothesis in a systematic and controlled way.

▶ Positivists use quantitative data to measure patterns of behaviour (e.g. suicide rates). This allows them to produce statements about the relationship between the facts they are investigating, and thereby discover laws of cause and effect.

Application
Use Durkheim's suicide study to illustrate the positivist approach. He explained patterns in suicide statistics as being caused by differences in the levels of integration and regulation.

▶ Positivists use methods that give maximum objectivity and detachment, i.e. quantitative methods such as experiments and official statistics.

Interpretivism

Interpretivists do not believe sociology can or should adopt the logic and methods of the natural sciences, because these are unsuited to the study of human beings.

▶ For interpretivists, sociology is about people's internal meanings, not external causes.

▶ Therefore sociology cannot be a science, because science only deals with laws of cause and effect, and not meanings.

▶ Because of this, interpretivists reject the use of natural science methods and causal explanations.

The subject matter of sociology

Interpretivists argue that there is a fundamental difference between the subject matter of the natural sciences and that of sociology.

▶ Natural science studies matter, which has no consciousness. Its behaviour is an automatic reaction to an external stimulus; matter doesn't choose how to act.

▶ Sociology studies people, who *do* have consciousness and choice. People make sense of their world by attaching meanings to it and these are internal to their consciousness.

▶ Individuals are not puppets manipulated by external 'social facts', but autonomous beings who construct their social world through the meanings they give to it.

Interpretivist methods

▶ The purpose of sociology is to uncover these meanings.

▶ Interpretivists argue that to discover the meanings people hold, we need to see the world from their viewpoint using what Weber calls *verstehen* (empathetic understanding) to grasp their meanings.

Two versions of interpretivism

▶ **Interactionists** believe we *can* have causal explanations, but through a 'bottom-up' approach, or *grounded theory*. Rather than entering the research with a fixed hypothesis, as positivists do, ideas emerge gradually from the observations made.

▶ **Phenomenologists and ethnomethodologists** such as Atkinson completely reject the possibility of causal explanations of human behaviour. Their radically anti-structural view argues that society is not a real thing 'out there'.

Postmodernism and feminism

Postmodernists also reject natural science as a model for sociology, because they see it as merely a meta-narrative – just somebody's 'big story' – not as 'the truth'.

▶ Science's account of the world is no more valid than any other, so there is no reason why science should be the model for sociology.

▶ Furthermore, a scientific approach is dangerous because it claims a monopoly of the truth and excludes other points of view – it is a form of domination.

▶ Poststructuralist feminists share this view of scientific sociology. The quest for a single, scientific feminist theory is a form of domination, since it excludes many groups of women.

What is science?

Positivists see natural science as inductive reasoning or verificationism applied to the study of observable patterns. However, not everyone accepts the positivists' portrayal of the natural sciences and there are three major alternative views.

Karl Popper: how science grows

Popper poses two questions: what makes scientific knowledge unique? And why has scientific knowledge grown so spectacularly in just a few centuries?

▶ Popper rejects the positivist view that science is based on verificationism: the idea that we can prove a theory true by gathering evidence that supports it.

▶ Instead, what makes science unique is the opposite of verificationism – the principle of falsificationism. This is the idea that a statement is scientific if it is capable of being falsified (disproved) by the evidence.

▶ A good theory therefore is one that (a) is in principle falsifiable *but*, when tested, in fact stands up to all attempts to disprove it and (b) explains a great deal.

Analysis
This is why interpretivists favour the use of qualitative methods and data such as PO, which give the sociologist a subjective understanding of the actor's life-world.

Evaluation
Atkinson's ethnomethodological study of suicide rejects the positivist idea that social facts outside the individual determine suicide rates. Suicide statistics are social constructs, not social facts as Durkheim claims.

Interpretation
Explain this claim in terms of science not always leading to the progress that positivists believed it would, e.g. 'risk society'.

Application
Illustrate the problem with verificationism with the 'all swans are white' claim. We can gather supporting evidence very easily (many swans *are* white), but a single observation of a black swan destroys the theory.

▶ All knowledge is provisional – there can never be absolute proof that any knowledge is true. A theory that *appears* true is simply one that has withstood attempts to falsify it so *far*.

▶ For a theory to be falsifiable, it must be open to criticism from other scientists so that its flaws can be exposed and better theories developed.

Implications for sociology

▶ Much sociology is unscientific because its theories could not under any circumstances be proved false, e.g. Marx's prediction that there will be a revolution – some day.

▶ However, sociology *can* be scientific by producing hypotheses that could be tested and in principle falsified.

▶ Popper acknowledges that sociological ideas may be of value because they may become testable at some later date and meanwhile can still be examined for clarity and logical consistency.

Analysis
Popper argues that science thrives in 'open', liberal societies that believe in free expression, but not in ones with closed belief systems such as totalitarian states or ones dominated by religion.

Thomas Kuhn: scientific paradigms

A paradigm is a shared framework held by members of a given scientific community – a kind of culture.

▶ The paradigm defines what their science is and provides them with a set of shared basic assumptions, principles and methods that allows them to do productive work.

▶ Scientists are socialised into the paradigm through their education and training, and come to accept it uncritically as true.

▶ A science cannot exist without a shared paradigm. Without one, there will only be rival schools of thought or perspectives, not a unified science.

▶ **Normal science** For most of the time, the paradigm goes unquestioned and scientists do 'puzzle solving' within the paradigm. This allows the scientific community to accumulate knowledge.

▶ **Anomalies** However, from time to time, scientists obtain findings contrary to those predicted by the paradigm. If too many such anomalies are found, confidence in the paradigm declines.

▶ **Crisis** The science enters a period of crisis and scientists begin to formulate rival paradigms.

▶ **Scientific revolution** Eventually, one paradigm wins out and becomes accepted by the scientific community, allowing normal science to resume, but with a new set of basic assumptions and principles.

Analysis
Contrast Kuhn's view of science as puzzle-solving within a paradigm with Popper's view of falsification as the unique feature of science.

Evaluation
This rejects Popper's view of the scientific community as open, critical and rational – Kuhn sees scientists as essentially conformists, blinkered by the paradigm.

Implications for sociology

▶ Sociology is divided into competing perspectives so it is currently pre-paradigmatic and pre-scientific according to Kuhn's model of science.

▶ Sociology could only become a science if such disagreements were resolved and whether this is even *possible* is open to doubt; e.g. even *within* perspectives, there are often disagreements.

▶ Postmodernists argue that a paradigm would also not be *desirable* in sociology – too much like a meta-narrative.

Realism and science

Realists such as Keat and Urry stress the similarities between sociology and certain kinds of natural science in terms of the degree of control the researcher has over the variables being researched.

Closed systems are those where the researcher can control and measure all the relevant variables and make precise predictions, e.g. through laboratory experiments.

Open systems are those where the researcher cannot control and measure all the relevant variables and so cannot make precise predictions.

▶ Sociologists study open systems where the processes are too complex or large-scale to make exact predictions.

▶ Realists reject the positivist view that science is only concerned with observable phenomena; e.g. physicists cannot directly observe the interior of a black hole in space, but they can still study it.

▶ Both natural and social science attempt to explain the causes of events in terms of underlying structures by observing their effects; e.g. we cannot directly see 'social class', but we can observe its effects on people's life chances.

▶ Unlike interpretivists, therefore, realists see little difference between natural science and sociology, except that some natural scientists are able to study closed systems under laboratory conditions.

Application
Apply this view to the interpretivist assumption that sociology cannot be scientific because actors' meanings are not observable. Realists say this is no barrier to studying meanings scientifically.

Interpretation
Explain how in this view, much sociology is scientific because it sees underlying structures such as capitalism producing effects such as poverty.

ONE TO TRY

Question Assess the arguments for and against the view that sociology is not and will never be a scientific discipline.   (33 marks)

Examiner's Advice There are two issues here: is sociology currently a science, and could it ever become one? It's worth stating at the outset that there are different views of what science is and that this will affect whether we think sociology is or could ever be a science. Then explain how positivists favour the natural sciences as a model and see sociology as scientific, but interpretivists reject this because of the nature of sociology's subject matter, as well as postmodernist and feminist criticisms of the positivists' choice of natural science as a model. Next explain that the debate so far has assumed that the natural sciences are as the positivists claim, but that there are other views of what science is, such as Popper, Kuhn and realism. Go on to examine these views and the implications of each view for whether sociology is a science currently or what it would need to do to become a science in future.

8 Sociology and social policy

Key Issues

▶ What is the difference between social problems and sociological problems?

▶ What factors may affect the extent to which sociology can influence social policy?

▶ What are the strengths and limitations of the main sociological perspectives on the relationship between sociology and social policy?

Social problems and sociological problems

▶ **A social problem** is some piece of social behaviour that causes public and/or private misery and calls for collective action to solve it, e.g. poverty or crime.

▶ **A sociological problem** is any pattern of relationships that calls for sociological explanation.

▶ The two overlap, but a sociological problem can also include behaviour that society doesn't normally regard as a problem, e.g. why people are law-abiding.

▶ Many sociologists are interested in solving social problems through their research; e.g. sociologists who feel strongly about poverty or inequality have conducted research aimed at discovering solutions to these social problems.

▶ Some sociologists are employed by government departments such as the Home Office or the Department of Education, often having a direct input into policy-making.

> **Analysis**
>
> For sociologists, 'normal' behaviour is just as interesting and just as much in need of an explanation as behaviour that people see as a 'social problem'.

The influence of sociology on policy

▶ Even when sociologists conduct research into social problems, there is no guarantee that government policy-makers will take act on their findings.

▶ Many factors affect whether or not policy-makers use sociologists' research findings to shape their policies. These include electoral popularity, how far the researcher's value-stance matches the government's political ideology, the cost of implementing proposals, support or opposition from interest groups, and the possibility that critical sociology (e.g. Marxism) may be regarded as too extreme.

> **Application**
>
> Apply examples of policies that might be affected by some of these factors; e.g. research may support a minimum wage to reduce poverty, but business interest groups may campaign against it.

Perspectives on social policy and sociology

There are different views of the nature of the state and social policy and of the role of sociology in relation to social policy.

1 Positivism and functionalism

▶ **Early positivists** saw sociology as a science that would both discover the cause of social problems and provide their solutions. Science and reason could be used to improve society.

▶ **Functionalists** see society as based on value consensus, so the state serves the interests of society as a whole, implementing rational social policies for the good of all.

▶ For both functionalists and positivists, the sociologist's role is to provide the state with objective, scientific information on which it can base its policies.

▶ Functionalists favour policies that are sometimes referred to as 'piecemeal social engineering' – cautious, bit-by-bit change rather than wholesale change.

> **Application**
>
> For example, Durkheim's analysis led him to propose a meritocratic education system to promote social cohesion by fostering a sense that society was fair.

2 The social democratic perspective

▶ The social democratic perspective on social policy favours a major redistribution of wealth and income from the rich to the poor.

▶ Sociologists should be involved in researching social problems and making policy recommendations to eradicate them. Townsend's research on poverty has led him to make recommendations for policies such as fairer, higher benefit levels.

3 Postmodernism

▶ For postmodernists, it is impossible to discover objective truth. All knowledge produced by research is uncertain, and so sociological findings cannot provide a satisfactory basis for policy-making.

▶ Sociologists can only take the role of 'interpreters', offering one view of reality among many, and not the role of 'legislators' (law-makers).

4 Marxism

In the Marxist view, social policies serve the interests of capitalism, not those of society as a whole.

▶ Social policies provide ideological legitimation for capitalism; e.g. the welfare state gives it a 'human face'.

▶ They maintain the labour force for further exploitation; e.g. the NHS keeps workers fit enough to work.

▶ They are a means of preventing revolution; e.g. the creation of the welfare state was a way of buying off working-class opposition to capitalism.

▶ For Marxists, the sociologist's role should thus be to reveal the exploitation that underpins capitalism and the way in which the ruling class use social policies to mask this.

5 Feminism

Feminists see society as patriarchal, benefiting men at women's expense. They see the state's social policies perpetuating women's subordination.

▶ Research by liberal feminists has had an impact in a number of policy areas; e.g. anti-discrimination and equal pay policies.

▶ Some radical feminist ideas have also had an influence on social policy, e.g. the establishment of women's refuges for women escaping domestic violence.

▶ However, many Marxist and radical feminists reject the view that reformist social policies can liberate women and call for more radical changes that the existing state cannot deliver.

6 The New Right

The New Right believe that the state should have only limited involvement in society; e.g. state welfare provision should be minimal.

▶ State intervention undermines people's sense of responsibility, leading to greater social problems.

▶ Murray argues that policies such as welfare benefits and council housing for lone parents act as 'perverse incentives' that encourage a dependency culture.

▶ The New Right see the role of sociologists as being to propose policies that promote individual responsibility and choice.

▶ The New Right support a strong 'law and order' policy and research by right realist criminologists, e.g. *Broken Windows*, has been influential in the introduction of zero tolerance policies.

ONE TO TRY

Question Assess different views of the relationship between sociology and social policy. (33 marks)

Examiner's Advice Start by clearly differentiating between sociological problems and social problems. You can then make use of the full range of views of the relationship between sociology and social policy including positivist, functionalist, Marxist, social democratic, feminist, New Right and postmodernism. Link these perspectives to key questions such as whether sociology is or should be closely related to social policy. You could also consider some of the factors that might prevent sociology influencing policy, such as cost, the government's political ideology etc.

Practice question and student answer

Question

Evaluate the contribution made by feminist sociologists to our understanding of contemporary society.

(33 marks)

Student answer by Moira

> A reasonable start, but could 'unpack' the idea of the Enlightenment project a bit, and say more about gender inequality as central to feminist concerns.

Like many other sociological perspectives, feminists apply the logic of the 18th century Enlightenment project to their approach – they believe that through rationality, we can rid society of gender inequality. However, there are several types of feminism, each of which has its own view of the nature of women's oppression.

> Some potentially relevant knowledge here on rights, sex/gender and domestic labour, but needs to say more – especially about piecemeal reforms.

Liberal feminists are concerned with patriarchy (male domination) and with women's rights in society. Ann Oakley makes an important distinction between sex and gender. In her view, sex refers to biological differences between male and female, whereas gender refers to how femininity and masculinity are regarded by society. The role of a woman doing unpaid domestic labour is imposed by their femininity – patriarchal society believes that expressive roles can only be performed by women, therefore patriarchy oppresses them by keeping them at home doing childcare and housework. Liberal feminists seek to abolish this idea through gradual change and piecemeal reforms.

> Moira shows understanding of the basic idea behind radical feminism, but should develop it by exploring its key concepts.

Radical feminists have a more extreme form of feminism. They take the view that men are the main enemy and that everything negative about society has been brought about by men. They believe today's society is a patriarchal one and needs to be abolished.

> A fairly good account of radical feminism's strategies for change – but could also talk about its contribution to understanding issues such as domestic violence and pornography.

Radical feminists have three main strategies to achieve this: create all-female households, create more support groups for subordinated women and promote lesbianism as the only non-oppressive type of relationship. They also call for the same marriage rights that heterosexual couples have. Radical feminists believe that women in heterosexual relationships are 'sleeping with the enemy'. In contrast to liberal feminists, they see change happening as a result of revolution and political pressure.

> Rather brief, but identifies some functions of women's oppression and explains 'familism'. Not accurate enough on the similarities and differences with radical feminism, though.

Like all feminists, Marxist feminists draw on the idea of patriarchy, but also use the Marxist view of capitalism. They believe that the oppression of women has ideological functions for capitalist society. These include absorbing men's anger, reproducing the labour force and providing a stable home environment. Barrett, a Marxist feminist, uses the term 'ideology of familism' to describe why women accept their subordination. Familism means that women have accepted that unpaid domestic labour is the natural thing for them to do to achieve fulfilment. Like radical feminists, they believe in the need for revolution and that the overthrow of capitalism will liberate women.

> Too brief, and not a very clear or accurate account of this type of feminism. The criticism could be applied more usefully to Marxist feminism.

Dual systems feminists combine the ideas of radical feminism and Marxist feminism. They think that because capitalism is male dominated, it is inevitable that women will be controlled by men. However, dual systems feminists have been criticised, because not all capitalist societies have high levels of gender inequality, e.g. Sweden, where men and women are more equal.

> Good awareness of some of the changes to women's position in contemporary society and the impact of feminism as a political movement – but not really about its contribution to *understanding* today's society.

> The first two sentences need developing. The answer would have been better off *without* the last sentence.

In conclusion, since the women's liberation movement of the 1960s and 1970s, women's welfare and interests have come much more to the forefront of society and women are now more aware of their rights. We can thank feminism for the opportunities that women have today, such as equal pay, job opportunities and the right to vote. Although women are still under-represented in the political system, it is steadily improving and as more women reach a position to change the laws, women's lives should improve further.

However, feminists can be criticised for having such a narrow interest. Feminism tends to ignore age, ethnicity and class, and therefore is not suitable for studying society as a whole. Combining feminism with other perspectives such as functionalism, Marxism and postmodernism would give a far better understanding of today's society.

How to turn this into a top-mark answer

Knowledge
Moira has a reasonable knowledge of some of the main versions of feminism – although she is weak on dual systems theory, and could at least mention one or two others, such as black or difference feminism. Her account of the types that she does deal with could also be developed further by including more concepts and issues. For example:
- On liberal feminism, she could say more about legislation and changes in attitudes or socialisation.
- On Marxist feminism, concepts such as the reserve army of labour and reproduction of the labour force could appear.
- On radical feminism, concepts of separatism, consciousness raising and 'the personal is political' would be useful.

Interpretation and Application
The question is about 'contemporary society', so you should include some material on how feminism helps (or fails to help) us understand areas such as families and households, education, crime etc. You should therefore illustrate your answer by applying material from feminist studies of such areas. Although Moira does talk about feminism in relation to changes in women's position, this is about feminism as a political movement, not as a sociological explanation of these changes.

You could also say something about why many feminists prefer qualitative research methods.

Analysis and Evaluation
A good way to show the skill of Analysis in this question would be to compare and contrast the different types of feminism. Pointing out the similarities and differences between them can also pave the way to some Evaluation by identifying what each approach has missed. Moira makes a start on this at the end of paragraphs two and three, but she doesn't take it very far. You could develop it for example by considering what *kinds* of revolution Marxist feminists and radical feminists want.

Conclusion
Moira's conclusion – especially the last, throwaway sentence – leaves a bad final impression. Avoid this 'a combination of all the different perspectives will give us the truth' ending unless you can actually *justify* it (the chances are you won't be able to).

Practice Paper for Unit 3

Read Item A and answer the questions that follow.

Item A

One important aspect of the secularisation debate is the extent of religious belief in society. However, there are problems in defining what we mean by both 'religious' and 'belief'. For example, should civil religion and political ideologies that act in similar ways to religion be included?

Even if a definition can be agreed, there are further difficulties of measurement. As belief cannot be directly observed, researchers have often used surveys to ask questions about people's personal religious beliefs. However, there are several problems involved in relying on this approach.

1   Identify and briefly explain **three** functions that religion could be said to carry out.   (9 marks)

2   Using material from **Item A** and elsewhere, assess the difficulties that sociologists face in trying to measure religious belief.   (18 marks)

3   'Religious belief, membership and practice all vary by ethnicity, gender, class and age.'

    Critically examine the arguments and evidence surrounding this view.   (33 marks)

Practice Paper for Unit 4

Note: this paper is based on the format to be used for Unit 4 papers from January 2012 onwards. See the note on page 126 for details of the format for the 2011 papers.

Answer all the questions.

Question 1

Using material from **Item A** and elsewhere, assess sociological explanations of the reasons for ethnic differences in recorded crime rates.

(21 marks)

Item A

Official statistics show striking differences between ethnic groups in relation to crime and the law. For example, compared with white people, black people are seven times more likely to be stopped and searched by police, three and a half times more likely to be arrested, and five times more likely to be in prison.

Some sociologists argue that such patterns are largely the result of real differences in the rates of crime committed by members of different ethnic groups. However, others argue that they are mainly the product of discrimination in the criminal justice system.

Question 2

Using material from **Item B** and elsewhere, assess sociological explanations of media representations of crime and their effects.

(21 marks)

Item B

In today's society, we learn about crime and deviance largely from the mass media. Unfortunately, however, the image we are given is often an inaccurate one. While we might expect fictional portrayals of crime – in films, on TV, in novels and so on – not to be an accurate representation, many sociologists argue that the image presented via the news media also distorts the reality of crime.

Sociologists are very interested both in the possible causes of these misrepresentations, and also in the effects that they may have on deviant behaviour.

Question 3

Using material from **Item C** and elsewhere, assess the strengths and limitations of using observation to research street crime.

(15 marks)

Item C

Street crime is a loose term for criminal offences that take place in public places. The Metropolitan Police describe street crime as "robbery, often called 'mugging', and also including thefts from victims in the street where property is snatched and the victim is not assaulted".

Observing street crime is problematic as 'the streets' are an ill-defined, potentially open-ended research context. In such a setting, it would be impossible for a researcher working alone to observe everything that is going on. Furthermore, street crime is difficult to predict, often violent and can be over very quickly.

Question 4

Assess the contribution of symbolic interactionism to our understanding of society.

(33 marks)

Top Marks Answers for Unit 3

The following answers to the Unit 3 Practice Paper questions on page 116 all scored full marks.

Answer to Question 1

One function religion performs is integration. Functionalists argue that religion binds us together by setting out agreed norms and values. The Ten Commandments lay down a basic moral code that all members of society can live by. Without this shared code, social life would be unregulated and society would fragment.

For Marxists, another function of religion is to legitimate capitalism. It justifies the inequalities that capitalism creates by saying they are God's will and offering spiritual comfort to the poor with promises of rewards in heaven. This creates a false consciousness that reconciles them to their poverty and makes it less likely that they will blame capitalism for their misery.

Thirdly, religion provides people with help and support in times of crisis. Parsons argued that religion provides an explanation for events that we cannot control such as death and bereavement. Suggesting that these are God's will helps people to cope with their grief and loss.

$\frac{9}{9}$

> **Examiner's Comments**
> Three clear and developed answers. The explanatory development of each point is crucial to gaining the six AO2 marks for this question.

Answer to Question 2

Measuring religious belief is important because it can tell us a great deal about religion's role and social significance. However, there are many difficulties involved in measuring something so abstract and hard to define. For example, sociologists sometimes use quantitative data from opinion poll surveys on belief in aspects of the supernatural to measure the extent of religious belief in society. However, this poses problems. For example, a question such as 'Do you believe in God' may mean very different things to different people, so responses may be of little real sociological value.

There may also be a tendency for respondents to claim to hold beliefs that they do not hold or that have little influence on their lives. This may be because they regard it as respectable or socially expected to be a believer.

Sociologists sometimes try to estimate the extent of belief by examining levels of participation in religious activities such as church attendance. However, participation is not the same thing as belief. A good illustration of this is how church attendance statistics can be interpreted in opposed ways. Secularisation theorists interpret falling attendance rates as a sign of the decline in levels of belief. However, if Herberg's view of religion in the USA is correct, the churches themselves have become secularised, so high attendance rates may not be a sign of the revival of religious belief at all.

Although not all sociologists accept Herberg's thesis, it does illustrate the problem of using quantitative data on attendance to try to measure belief. Likewise, while Davie argues that we now have 'believing without belonging', i.e. without ever attending a place of worship, Bruce argues that these are not 'true believers' at all, but rather a sign of the weakening of religious belief and commitment.

Sociologists interested in testing the secularisation thesis often seek to make historical comparisons to discover whether or not the level of belief is falling. However, this raises the problem of measuring past levels of belief. Survey data does not exist before the relatively recent past and attendance figures from previous centuries are open to problems of interpretation – did people go to church out of belief, or out of conformity and social pressure?

Finally, any attempt to measure religious belief comes up against the problem of distinguishing religious from non-religious beliefs. What counts as a specifically 'religious' belief – e.g. belief in astrology or UFOs? There are several ways to define religion; therefore, depending upon whether we use an 'inclusive' (wide, e.g. including civil religion referred to in Item A) definition or an 'exclusive' (narrow) one, the level of religious belief can seem to vary greatly.

Thus there are two problems here, that of defining 'belief 'and that of defining 'religion'. This is important because how we define each concept will have a major effect on what the level of religious belief appears to be when we measure it. This in turn influences how we answer important questions about the strength of religion in today's society. $\binom{18}{18}$

> **Examiner's Comments**
> This is a thorough and focused answer that deals with a range of problems involved in defining and measuring religious belief. It examines opinion polling, the relevance of church attendance, the interpretation of statistics, the historical dimension and the definition of religiosity. There is also an effective concluding paragraph.

Answer to Question 3

There is considerable evidence for the view that different groups have different patterns of religious belief, practice and membership. For example, in terms of class, Weber and Troeltsch both argued that the poor and marginalised were likely to be attracted to sects (like Wallis' world-rejecting new religious movements). For Weber, this was because they offered a 'theodicy of disprivilege' – an explanation of their disadvantaged status – and what Stark and Bainbridge call 'compensators' or the promise of religious rewards for their suffering. This is similar to millenarian movements that appeal to colonised peoples in Third World countries and to the Christian idea that 'the meek shall inherit the earth'.

However, while marginality may explain lower-class recruitment to sects, some middle-class people are also attracted to such movements. One reason may be relative deprivation – the subjective sense of being deprived compared to others. However, the middle class may often be attracted to world-affirming rather than world-rejecting beliefs and organisations. Similarly, compared with the working class, the higher classes are more likely to be members of churches rather than sects. According to Troeltsch, this reflects the fact that churches have more conservative beliefs, which appeals to the better off, while sects tend to be more revolutionary and opposed to the social status quo, which appeals to the poor.

Some of these points also apply to ethnic differences. In societies where ethnic minorities are discriminated against or feel like outsiders, religion may be a source of support. Thus in Britain, levels of belief and practice are higher among Hindus, Muslims and Black Christians than among whites. Bruce argues that this is because of cultural defence: religion provides a sense of identity and a way of preserving one's culture in an often racist society. It also eases cultural transition into the new society by providing a sense of community. Once the transition has been made, levels of religiosity fall, so if minorities become assimilated, we should expect differences in levels of belief and practice to even out too.

Another explanation of ethnic differences is that most minorities in Britain come from countries where religion is more important and so they are just carrying over the beliefs and practices of their country of origin. Finally, regarding Black Christians, many found themselves shunned by the mainstream, white-dominated British churches and turned instead to Pentecostalism.

Regarding gender, women are more likely than men to hold religious beliefs and engage in religious practice. Miller and Hoffmann found this true of all age groups and all faiths. One reason is gender role differences: women are socialised to be more passive and obedient – qualities valued by most religions. Similarly, Greeley argues that women's caring role increases religiosity because it involves responsibility for the 'ultimate' welfare of others. Women's gender role also means they are less likely to work full-time and so have more opportunity to participate in religious activity.

Heelas and Woodhead found 80% of the 'holistic milieu' were female and some features of the New Age make it especially attractive to women, such as its 'expressive' emphasis, e.g. on healing – traditionally a female role. Likewise, its values of 'authenticity' and 'autonomy' may appeal to women restricted by patriarchal definitions of their gender role. Also, the fact that women are generally poorer may explain why more women than men join sects. All this may help to explain both why women are more likely to be active members, and why they hold different kinds of religious belief from men; e.g. a belief in God as love rather than as power.

Age differences also play a part in patterns of belief, practice and membership: children and the elderly have the highest participation rates. One reason may be that the old have the time (unlike those of working age or rearing a family), while the young may be made to attend by their parents. Another possible reason is that the old are nearer to death and so more concerned with issues such as immortality. However, it has been noted that secularisation means that each generation is less religious than the one before it, so the old may just be more religious because they grew up at a time when everyone was more religious.

One notable exception to the trend in age and religion is the Pentecostal churches, which continue to attract younger people. However, this may be more to do with ethnicity than age – Pentecostalism may be a form of cultural defence or transition for young Black people. This also shows that every individual has a class, gender, ethnicity and age, and that these factors can interact in different ways, leading to different patterns of religious belief and practice for different people.

$\frac{33}{33}$

Examiner's Comments
This is a comprehensive answer that deals with all the groups in the question. It shows a detailed knowledge of a range of relevant facts, studies and concepts, and offers alternative explanations as the basis for developing appropriate evaluation.

Top Marks Answers for Unit 4

The following answers to the Unit 4 Practice Paper questions on page 117 all scored full marks.

Answer to Question 1

As Item A indicates, there are important differences in the experience of ethnic groups in the criminal justice system. For example, in addition to differences in the stop and search, arrest and imprisonment rates described in the Item, Asians are three times more likely than others to be stopped under anti-terrorism laws.

There are two broad explanations for such patterns. As Item A notes, some see them as the result of higher rates of offending among minorities, especially blacks, whereas others see them as resulting from racism in the criminal justice system (CJS) such as police and courts. Which (if any) of these explanations is true?

Right realists such as Murray argue that blacks do have a higher rate of offending. He argues that black boys are more likely to be brought up in lone-parent, welfare-dependent 'underclass' families that lack a father who works to support his family and imposes discipline on his children. Instead, boys are left to look to delinquent street gangs for role models and status. However, even if this is true, it doesn't explain why black boys should be more likely to be brought up in lone-parent families in the first place.

Left realists such as Kinsey, Lea and Young agree that blacks have a higher rate of offending. However, they argue that this is because ethnic minorities are more likely to be socially excluded from opportunities to achieve legitimately as a result of discrimination in education, employment and housing. This gives rise to feelings of relative deprivation – of unfairly having less than others. At the same time, they experience the same pressure as everyone else to achieve the material goods that society tells us to aspire to.

One response is to join subcultures. Some may join religious subcultures, but others join criminal subcultures. Their marginalisation means they lack the organisation to achieve material success by lawful means. Others express their frustration through violence and rioting.

By contrast, neo-Marxists argue that ethnic differences in offending are not a fact, but a social construct. This approach draws on interactionism to argue that the CJS negatively labels minorities, resulting in higher rates of arrest and conviction and harsher sentences. For example, Hood found that black and Asian men received longer sentences than whites for offences of similar seriousness. Blacks are also more likely than whites to die in police custody.

Thus the neo-Marxist Gilroy argues that black criminality is a 'myth' created by racist stereotypes; blacks are no more criminal than others. He argues that their only crime is to engage in political struggle to resist a racist society, using methods such as riots and demonstrations that their parents had used to resist oppression in the British colonies from which they came. The British state then criminalised this behaviour.

However, Lea and Young criticise this. They argue that because first generation immigrants were law-abiding, it is unlikely that they passed on a tradition of anti-colonial struggle; that most crime is within ethnic groups, not an anti-racist struggle, and that Gilroy romanticises street crime as political. Also, Asians' crime rates are similar to or lower than whites', so this would mean the police are only racist towards blacks, not other minorities.

Hall et al also argue that black crime is a social construct. They claim that in times of capitalist crisis, such as the 1970s, the ruling class need to legitimate the use of more authoritarian forms of rule, e.g. to suppress opposition. In the 1970s, a media-driven moral panic about the supposed growth of 'mugging' committed by black youths was used to do this. In reality, they argue, there was no significant increase in street robberies, but the myth of the black mugger served as a scapegoat to deflect attention from the real cause of the crisis – capitalism – and divide the working class on racial lines.

Hall et al combine Marxism (the capitalist crisis) with labelling theory (stereotyping of blacks) to explain ethnic differences in crime rates as a construct. However, they are inconsistent – they argue that there was no increase in black crime, but also that there was, as a result of rising unemployment. On the other hand, their approach helps to explain why Asians have a lower crime rate than blacks, since they were not scapegoated in this way. Likewise, recent rises in Asians' rates may be the result of their now being labelled as 'terrorists' since 9/11.

$\frac{21}{21}$

> ### Examiner's Comments
> This is a thorough answer that covers the recorded patterns of ethnic differences, both from the Item and elsewhere. It presents three major explanations (right realist, left realist and neo-Marxist), using a range of relevant concepts, and evaluates the theories it puts forward. It would benefit from a conclusion, but nevertheless is well worth full marks.

Answer to Question 2

Crime is a recurring subject in the media. Content analysis shows that newspapers and TV news broadcasts dedicate a large amount of space and time to crime. But as Item B notes, media depictions distort our view of crime. For example, in fiction the typical offender is older and higher-class than in the statistics and policing is represented as more successful than is really the case. Likewise, the type of crime portrayed in both fiction and the news is untypical of 'real life' crime, at least according to official statistics and victim surveys. Violent crime is over-represented, property crime under-represented, risks of victimisation exaggerated, and sex crimes are committed by psychopathic strangers. Surette calls this 'the law of opposites' – the media picture is the opposite of reality.

A major cause of these misrepresentations is news values – the criteria by which journalists decide what stories to include. As Cohen and Young point out, news is not discovered but 'manufactured' or socially constructed, and news values such as risk, violence, dramatisation and personalisation help determine whether a crime story gets reported. One recent trend is for victimisation to become a more important news value – so crimes without an easily identifiable victim (e.g. corporate crime) go under-reported.

One possible effect of the media's emphasis on violence and victimisation is it leads to unrealistic fear of crime and this affects people's behaviour. For example, Schlesinger and Tumber found heavy users of TV were more afraid of going out at night and becoming a victim. However, it may be that those who are already afraid of going out watch more TV just because they stay in more. Nevertheless, according to the BCS, while crime is actually falling, fear of crime is rising, and this may be due to the media.

Another effect of media representations may be 'copycat' crime, where offenders imitate behaviour seen in the media. However, this is hard to test, partly because it is difficult to isolate the media from all the other possible variables that might cause crime, e.g. socialisation, poverty etc. Most attempts to test it have been via laboratory experiments, which lack validity due to their artificiality.

However, left realists Lea and Young argue that the media do encourage crime – not by portraying crime, but by portraying the materialistic goals that society wants us actually to conform to. By portraying the 'good life' of material goods, the media stimulate relative deprivation (the sense of having less than others), since people no longer compare themselves with their neighbours, but with high-living media celebrities. This also links with Merton's strain theory, where working-class people turn to 'innovation' when blocked opportunities prevent them from obtaining society's materialistic goals legitimately. It also relates to Young's idea that the media promote cultural inclusion (TV advertising shows everyone what the 'glittering prizes' are), but society promotes economic exclusion – the poor are marginalised and cannot achieve legitimately.

A final way that media representations may have an effect on deviance is through moral panics (exaggerated over-reactions by society) resulting in a deviance amplification spiral. According to Cohen, the media stereotype a group as a folk devil or threat to society's values, leading to calls by moral entrepreneurs for a crackdown. This may lead to a self-fulfilling prophecy. For example, setting up police drug squads led to more drug-taking being uncovered, so the problem appeared larger, leading to more efforts at control, in an upward spiral.

Cohen illustrates this with the mods and rockers. The media produced exaggerated and distorted reports of minor incidents and predicted 'worse to come'. By using symbols to stereotype and stigmatise the groups, it created clear identities for others to adopt and polarised the two groups, resulting in more conflict between them (a self-fulfilling prophecy). It also helped provoke a stronger control response from police and courts, further stigmatising the groups. However, McRobbie and Thornton argue that the concept of moral panics is less useful in late modern society, where media panics are now so routine that the public no longer take them seriously.

Thus we have seen how news values can influence the portrayal of crime as sensational, extraordinary and threatening. This representation of crime may promote deviance, either by stimulating desires for material goods that the poor cannot obtain legitimately, or via media-fuelled moral panics. All this indicates the centrality of the media to understanding crime and deviance today.

$\frac{21}{21}$

> **Examiner's Comments**
> This answer shows knowledge of a wide range of aspects of the relationship between crime and the media – fictional and news representations, news values, fear of crime, copycat crime, relative deprivation and moral panics – along with relevant studies and concepts. There is a good focus on the set question of the causes and possible effects of media representations, with explicit analysis and evaluation of these.

Answer to Question 3

As the street is a public space, there are no official gatekeepers restricting the sociologist's access. However, those involved in street crime are often very aware of what is going on on their 'turf' and so the arrival of a stranger showing an interest in their activities is likely to arouse their suspicion. However, the observer may overcome this problem if they have insider contacts.

However, unlike many of the offenders involved in street crime, sociologists are often middle-class and older, and these characteristics can be difficult to disguise. This might cause problems when trying to make insider contacts.

Street crime includes acts of theft and violence, such as 'mugging' and bag snatching, as well as drug dealing and consumption. The observer thus faces a dilemma: standing by, observing people being victimised without intervening or informing the police is ethically dubious – and yet reporting these acts would probably compromise the observer's research role and any relationship they may have developed with offenders. However, there may be a broader ethical justification for not intervening: if the research brings a better understanding of street crime, it may lead to more effective policies to deal with it.

As Item C indicates, 'the streets' are an ill-defined, potentially open-ended context and it would be impossible for a lone researcher to observe more than a tiny proportion of such crimes. The nature of street crime also makes it difficult to be in the right place for research purposes and to record what happens. It is also hard to know how representative the observed acts are of all such crime.

Some of those involved in street crime are likely to be young and there are particular ethical problems when dealing with under-16s. It is questionable whether young people can understand the implications of research well enough to give informed consent.

Observation of young people in particular should be overt because of their greater vulnerability. However, this makes the Hawthorne effect more likely to occur (subjects acting as they think the researcher wants them to), reducing the research's validity. However, given the generally poorer literacy of those involved in street crime, observation is a better approach than a written questionnaire.

There are also practical issues in terms of relationships with offenders. Being seen with known criminals may lead the police to distrust the observer: if they are not aware of the researcher's purpose, the police may suspect them of being involved in crime. By contrast, if the observer has informed the local police about their research, then being seen anywhere near a police station may arouse the suspicions of offenders. The police may also be concerned about the observer's safety and this could interfere with their observations.

Street crime often involves violence and thus there is a greater element of danger, as Venkatesh and Patrick both discovered when researching gangs. With covert observation, which involves misleading members of the group, there is a risk of violence against the researcher if their real identity is uncovered.

15/15

Examiner's Comments
This answer deals with a range of issues in relation to observation, such as ethics, access, representativeness, the Hawthorne effect, practical issues such as danger etc. However, what makes it a very good answer is that it links these issues to the research characteristics of street crime – e.g. that it often involves juveniles, may be violent, sudden and hard to predict, problems of relationships with police and offenders etc.

Answer to Question 4

Symbolic interactionism is one of several 'action' approaches in sociology. It sees society as constructed from the bottom up through micro level interactions, as opposed to structural approaches such as functionalism and Marxism. Action theories are more voluntaristic than these 'top down' perspectives that see individuals' thoughts and behaviour determined by the social structure. However, as we shall see, there are some deterministic aspects to interactionism too.

Interactionism focuses on how we create the social world through our interactions. According to Mead, we respond to the world by attaching meanings or symbols to those things that are significant to us. Unlike animals who respond to a stimulus in a fixed way by instinct, we have to interpret its meaning before we can act. For example, someone shaking their fist at us may be threatening or joking and we have to decide which before we know how to respond. This also means we choose our behaviour.

To interpret someone's meaning, we have to 'take the role of the other', seeing ourselves as they see us. We learn to do this through socialisation, first internalising 'significant others' (e.g. parents) and then later, 'the generalised other' (wider society).

For interactionists, meanings arise from interaction and can to some extent be negotiated and changed. Although we have internalised other people's expectations through socialisation, there is always some scope for free will and choice in how we perform our roles. This contrasts with approaches such as functionalism and structural Marxism, which see the individual as a puppet passively responding to the system's needs.

There are several versions of interactionism, but the best known is labelling theory. This applies three key concepts to social life. These are firstly, 'the definition of the situation' – the idea that if we believe something to be real, it will have real consequences. For example, Becker argues that if a teacher believes a pupil to be 'thick', they may treat them as if they are and give up trying to help them. This is a valuable concept in understanding under-achievement, as well as areas like crime – e.g. police stereotyping minorities and 'over-policing' them as a result.

The second key concept of labelling theory is Cooley's 'looking-glass self' – the idea that, through taking the role of the other, we come to see ourselves as others see us. This can lead to a self-fulfilling prophecy; e.g. where a pupil comes to see himself as he thinks the teacher sees him, he lives up to the label and fails.

Thirdly, labelling theory uses the concept of 'career' – the idea that we may progress through a series of statuses. Lemert applies this to the process of becoming a mental patient, where a person may start off as a 'pre-patient' with certain symptoms, through medical labelling, to in-patient, to discharge. The status 'mental patient' may become our master status, defining who we are. This idea has been applied to crime, where labelled offenders may end up seeking out the company of other offenders and joining a subculture that reinforces their deviant status.

While labelling theory is valuable in understanding interaction processes and their effects, Marxists criticise it for ignoring class inequality in explaining the origins of labels, while functionalists attack it for ignoring the influence of shared norms. Its micro level focus means it fails to take account of such wider structural factors. Labelling theory has also been criticised for determinism, because it sees the labels that others attach to us as dictating our identities and actions through a self-fulfilling prophecy.

An alternative interactionist approach is Goffman's dramaturgical model. This is based on an analogy between social interaction and theatre, and uses concepts such as 'script', 'props', 'backstage' etc. His basic idea is that interaction is a 'performance' where we seek to convince others (our 'audience') that we are what we claim to be. Thus a hospital doctor uses props like a stethoscope, white coat etc to manage other people's impressions of him. Goffman argues that there is a 'role distance' between our real selves and our roles. This implies that we don't always believe in the roles we are playing – we are literally 'acting', manipulating our audience into accepting an impression that conceals our true self.

The dramaturgical analogy throws light on some aspects of social interaction, e.g. in situations such as interviews we may put on an act to manage others' impressions of us. However, critics argue that it is just a loose collection of descriptive concepts, rather than an explanatory theory that enables us to predict behaviour.

Different perspectives often favour a particular methodology. Interactionists prefer qualitative methods such as participant observation, unstructured interviews and the analysis of documents such as diaries. This is because qualitative data is said to produce valid (authentic) data and allow the researcher to interpret people's meanings by verstehen– putting oneself in the other's place. This can be valuable when studying groups of which the researcher has little or no personal knowledge, because it allows them to develop hypotheses in the course of gathering the data. For example, unstructured interviews are like guided conversations, where the researcher can follow up new insights as they emerge. By contrast, quantitative methods such as questionnaires start out with a fixed schedule of questions, many of which may be irrelevant to the respondents' experiences.

However, positivists criticise interactionists' methods for their subjective, impressionistic and unscientific approach. Not only are they not reliable (not replicable) or representative (because of small, haphazard samples), they don't even produce valid data, since ultimately the sociologist has to interpret its meaning, and there is no guarantee that they have done so correctly.

In conclusion, interactionism's small scale, interpretivist methodology fits with its neglect of structural factors. Nevertheless, it has produced some important concepts for understanding the processes by which the social world is constructed and some valuable contributions in fields such as education and deviance.

(33/33)

> **Examiner's Comments**
> This is a comprehensive answer that deals well with the key concepts of interactionism, including both its labelling and dramaturgical versions. It shows how some of these concepts have been applied in areas such as education, mental illness and crime, and it examines the relationship between interactionism and qualitative research methods. Analysis and evaluation are explicit and well developed throughout the answer.

Note on the format of Unit 4 papers

The January 2011 and June 2011 papers have the following format:

- **Crime & Deviance:** a 12-mark 'Examine' question and a 21-mark 'Using material from the Item and elsewhere, assess' question.

- **Methods in Context:** a 9-mark 'Identify and briefly explain three' question and a 15-mark, 'Using material from the Item and elsewhere, assess' question.

- **Theory & Methods:** a 33-mark essay question.

From January 2012 onwards, the 12-mark and 9-mark questions above will be replaced by a 21-mark Crime & Deviance question. Papers from January 2012 onwards will follow the format of the practice paper on page 117.

Your Notes